THE FASTER LEARNING ORGANIZATION

ORGANIZATION

Gain and Sustain the Competitive Edge

Bob Guns
with
Kristin Anundsen

The Jossey-Bass Business & Management Series

Jossey-Bass Publishers • San Francisco

Contents

Editor's Preface

Much has been written about the impact of the Information Age on organizations. Executives, managers, and front-line workers alike regularly face overwhelming amounts of information. Most of us realize that learning—absorbing information, sifting through it, reflecting on it, and using it to spur creativity—has become a daily responsibility.

The organization that doesn't promote learning—especially fast learning—can't expect to compete successfully. Consider the speed with which your competitors copy or improve on your best ideas. Any competitive advantage achieved with an innovative product, for instance, is extremely short-lived. Your people have to be *continually* learning and experimenting so that they can come up with the next innovation before your competitors do.

Bob Guns's model of a *faster learning organization* links organizational learning to achieving competitive advantage. Although Bob was inspired by Arie de Geus's work on organizational learning, his model is uniquely his own.

One important attribute of the model is its wide applicability. Virtually any organization of any size and in any circumstances can implement it. This applicability, coupled with the quality of the content, made Bob's book a natural for the *Executive Briefing Series*.

Bob's message is easy to understand, and the methods he advocates won't break the bank. I believe that this book will capture your imagination immediately. It certainly captured mine.

Warren Bennis
Santa Monica, California

v

Author's Preface

"The only way to sustain competitive advantage is to ensure that your organization is learning faster than the competition." When I first encountered Arie de Geus's strategic insight some years ago in Peter Schwartz's book, *The Art of the Long View,* I almost fell out of my chair. All other strategic ideas I had worked with in preceding years seemed to fall by the wayside.

I waited for someone to write a book on this profound idea. No one did. I finally felt compelled to do what no one had yet done.

I used Arie's ideas as a springboard for my own concept of a faster learning organization or FLO. I developed a model for creating and maintaining a FLO. In this book I link that model to three specific strategies as well as particular methods, tactics, skills, and action ideas to turn a FLO into reality.

This book has been written for executives and senior managers—the people who will set the stage and initiate the start-up of a FLO. However, no part of the organization will remain untouched in implementing a FLO; executives, leaders, team members, and individual employees will all be affected. Continuing commitment from all these faster learners is needed to make the FLO work.

Certain people made significant contributions to my ideas and this book. I would like to acknowledge a few of them. Kristin Anundsen acted as a sounding board for the ideas, wording, and shape of this book. Her fast and convincing wordsmithing and editing provided both a conciseness and a liveliness to the book. I thank Kristin for her contribution.

Arie de Geus's thoughtful comments along the way have been both inspiring and supportive. A number of people provided ongoing encouragement: Bob Aron of

Motorola University, Glen Wise of Ciba-Geigy, Phil Noble of StorageTek, Cyril Gallimore of American Standard, Hubert Saint-Onge of the Canadian Imperial Bank of Commerce, and Otto Brodtrick of Statistics Canada.

Carol Nolde, my editor, has provided unwavering enthusiasm, support, and writing proficiency to move this project along. Thank you for acting as a true collaborator, Carol. JoAnn Padgett and Karla Swatek of Pfeiffer & Company have also turned this assignment into an exciting and worthwhile exercise. Many thanks.

Two other special groups deserve mention. The first is the FLO Reading Network, a group of executives and senior managers in Vancouver, British Columbia, whose lively participation in the background reading for this book helped me immensely: Murray Braem, Harold Copping, Bob Chartier, Dennis Day, Brian Nixon, Paul Standring, Brent Leigh, Allan Oas, and Gervase Bushe. The other group is continuing to conduct research with me on how groups and teams learn: Tom Kayser of Xerox and LouAnn Daly of Innovation Associates. I want to thank them for their enthusiastic dedication to our ongoing discovery.

The last acknowledgment is to my family and particularly to my wife, Veronica. During my creative surge, Veronica had to endure early risings and excited ramblings about what I was discovering. I hope that the cups of coffee I brought her at 4:00, 5:00, and 6:00 in the morning partially made up for her loss of sleep. She has been an exceptional partner, one whose contribution to this book, my work, and our business life and family life is immeasurable.

I would also like to acknowledge you, the reader, for your interest in the concept of a faster learning organization. After you read this book, I hope you will take the risk of trying one small idea from this book. One small idea. And build from there. I give you my heartiest support as you grapple with how to build your enterprise as a faster learning organization—the major challenge confronting all our organizations in the coming years.

Bob Guns
Summit, New Jersey

Foreword

This book is based on an idea that makes perfect sense: The only way for an organization to gain and sustain the competitive edge is to learn faster than its competitors. Bob Guns's model for creating and maintaining a *faster learning organization* isn't some esoteric theory that no company could comprehend or implement; it's something that a CEO could easily present to managers and managers to front-line workers. And an organization could be off and running as a "FLO" with very little financial outlay.

The action ideas that accompany the chapters are equally practical and useful. What I especially like about them is that they include ideas for people at all organizational levels, not just executives.

Learning is a personal responsibility. We all need to accept ownership for our own learning and performance. And each of us must be responsible for acquiring the capabilities necessary to meet performance expectations. This book shows us how.

There's another aspect of this book that I admire: its inspiring quality. Bob's zest for learning and his concern and understanding for learners are evident throughout. He knows that learning is difficult for many people, that they sometimes have to get beyond bad childhood experiences to discover that learning can be fun. Knowing that, he's able to present ways to approach reluctant learners and show them the positive side of learning.

Of course, others of us already share Bob's excitement about learning. And for us, this book is not just an important contribution to future organizational success, but a great read as well. Thanks, Bob.

Hubert Saint-Onge
Toronto

***K**ey Idea:*
The only way to gain and sustain the competitive edge is to ensure that your organization is learning faster than the competition.

THE POWER OF
FASTER LEARNING

---

*Sustainability ensures that the challenger will have a
sufficiently long period to close the market share gap
before the leader can imitate.*

Michael Porter,
Competitive Advantage

1

A few years ago, while on a learning journey of my
own, I had the good fortune to come across the ideas of
Arie de Geus, formerly coordinator of Group Planning
for Royal Dutch/Shell and a pioneer in organizational
learning. After reading his ideas, I became fascinated
with the concept of building a "faster learning organization" or FLO.

This chapter explores the connection between faster
learning and competitiveness. A FLO finds out faster than
its competition what works better, thereby gaining and
sustaining the competitive edge—the ability to generate
and maintain profit and market share. When your organization knows what works better, it can use that knowledge to create superior products and services that customers consistently choose.

To obtain hard data on the importance of faster learning, Calhoun Wick of Wick and Company and David Ulrich of the University of Michigan School of Business conducted a research project involving 48 organizations. The project results showed significant correlations between learning speed and competitiveness as well as between learning speed and innovation/organization speed.[1]

The great danger, particularly in these times, is the possibility that a competitor will change the ground rules of your industry's game. And because you're still playing by the old rules, the source of your competitive advantage might be wiped out.

Four routes, all dependent on learning faster than the competition, are open to your organization when it's faced with this danger: (1) *Learn faster* how to adapt to ground rules that have already changed. (2) *Learn faster* what the next change in ground rules will be and start preparing for it. (3) *Learn faster* how to develop a vigorous competitive strategy that will withstand significant change in the ground rules. (4) *Learn faster* how to change the ground rules to your advantage and preempt the competition.

LEARNING VS. PERFORMANCE

All organizations learn, but not all are learning based. Many are performance based, or focused on today: getting the order, processing it, shipping it quickly.

What's wrong with the performance-based approach? Nothing, as far as it goes. But these days it isn't enough.

> *Learning-based organizations focus on getting the job done better. They view learning as the best way to improve long-term performance.*

The learning-based organization willingly sacrifices today's performance for the sake of tomorrow's. The performance-based organization doesn't make this sacrifice, and for that reason its financials may look better in the short term. But several important factors create a different long-term picture:

♦ Today's performance is a product of yesterday's learning. Tomorrow's performance is a product of today's learning.

♦ Because the learning-based organization keeps reinvesting in learning, its performance steadily improves over time.

♦ Because the performance-based organization doesn't reinvest in learning, its performance eventually suffers.

WHY FASTER LEARNING SPECIFICALLY?

"Faster" does not mean "hurried up." Faster learning requires simpler and more efficient ways to learn, fewer steps in the learning process, and more attention paid to leveraging opportunities.

> *Faster learning may even involve slower, more reflective thinking in order to focus on what's important.*

A FLO quickly closes the performance gap between itself and performance-based competitors. Meanwhile, the learning gap between the FLO and competitors continues to increase. Over time the performance-based competitors find it more and more difficult to catch up—in either learning or performance.

Senior executives will "buy in" to faster learning if they realize that any initial reduction in performance will be short lived, whereas long-term improvement in performance is almost a certainty. But if you find that organization-wide application of faster learning isn't an option for your company at this time, consider applying the principles in an individual work group. When the group succeeds, adoption of the principles in other groups—and, eventually, throughout the organization—will be easier to accomplish.

The impact of the Information Age: More new information has been produced in the past 30 years than in the previous 5,000; a weekday edition of *The New York Times* contains more information than the average person of the 16th century would encounter in a lifetime; and the amount of available information now doubles every five years.[2]

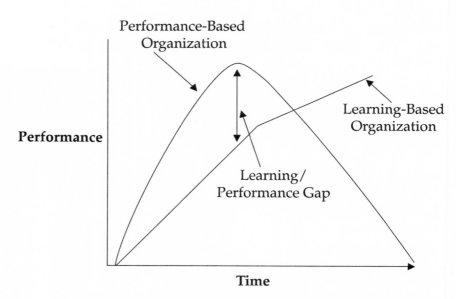

The Benefits of a Learning-Based Organization

CHARACTERISTICS OF A FLO

Faster learning propels an organization toward the lead in its industry because it enhances strategic capability, strengthens the organization's ability to change, and improves performance.

ENHANCES STRATEGIC CAPABILITY

Faster learning enhances an organization's strategic capability. The organization acts more realistically, focuses more steadily on its vision, and responds to industry changes more quickly than the competition.

1. Acts realistically. The FLO operates in a climate of openness. Employees give honest feedback to one another, react nondefensively, and exhibit an unflagging desire to improve. People at all levels are willing to discuss and work with the organizational reality.

2. Focuses on its vision. The FLO becomes extremely sensitive to its competitive position. The destination vision—what the organization will look like when it's sustaining the competitive edge—becomes paramount.

3. Responds to industry changes. The FLO anticipates changes in the industry ground rules and quickly figures out how to operate in accordance with those changes.

STRENGTHENS ABILITY TO CHANGE

A FLO strengthens its ability to change in light of new developments. It quickly acquires knowledge that customers value, uses new technology, reduces cycle time, innovates, exercises resiliency, and reinforces change.

Bill Gates, Microsoft CEO, an expert at responding to industry changes

1. Acquires knowledge that customers value. The FLO acts quickly to acquire new information, convert it into knowledge, and use that knowledge to provide increased value for customers.

2. Uses new technology to its advantage. The FLO learns about technological advancements quickly and applies them successfully to serve customers better.

3. Reduces cycle time. As Chris Meyer says in *Fast Cycle Time*, "Successful implementation of the FCT strategy requires a systemic integration of the new values, processes, goals, and rewards into the core work processes in order to increase the rate and speed of organizational learning." Learning must be targeted to adding value, as defined by end customers, and systematically improving the processes that deliver value.[3]

The FLO may discover that certain components of a process require even more time, whereas others can be shortened. The issue is to concentrate on reducing total cycle time, not the time consumed by individual process components. The organization determines

We live in an age in which speed and knowledge are the dynamics of success. The FLO combines these dynamics to create an unbeatable competitive force.

which components are most easily and readily shortened and focuses on those.

4. Innovates. Innovation thrives in an atmosphere of trust and risk taking. In a FLO, leaders cultivate trust by strongly supporting their employees. Risk taking naturally increases as employees eagerly strive to meet the challenges set out for them by their leaders.

5. Exercises resiliency. Learning is both a product of change and a catalyst for it. As a FLO develops its learning abilities, it becomes more resilient—more confident and more capable of handling further changes.

6. Reinforces change. The strategies, tactics, skills, and measurement tools used by a FLO can enhance any organizational-change effort, such as total quality management or reengineering. The learning associated with a change effort will occur quickly, be assimilated into the organization, and be transferred to those involved in other change projects.

*E*ven if you're on the right track, you'll get run over if you just sit there.

—Will Rogers

IMPROVES PERFORMANCE

A FLO focuses on improvement and runs each team as a small business, thereby enhancing performance.

1. Focuses on improvement. Performance improvement occurs in two ways, in small increments and in huge leaps known as breakthroughs. The leaders of a FLO cultivate this dual perspective by concentrating on details as well as the big picture. Moreover, employees recognize that there's no learning without application—that is, targeted performance improvement.

2. Runs teams as businesses. FLO teams are entrepreneurial; they run themselves as micro-businesses delivering to a bottom line. After they've reached world-class quality internally, they are spun off as separate organizations, where they can meet the needs of global customers within a narrow market niche.

THE FLO MODEL

On the next page is an illustration of the FLO Model. The following paragraphs briefly describe the dimensions of the model; later chapters expand these descriptions.

> *The FLO Model helps every employee or group move up at least one rung on the learning ladder.*

That kind of collective learning development has a profound long-term impact on the organization's performance.

VISION

The FLO is motivated by a strong vision: to gain and sustain the competitive edge through faster learning.

STRATEGIES

Strategies are plans for realizing the vision. Three strategies are required, each led by a different group: the *Surge Strategy*, led by the executive group; the *Cultivate Strategy*, led by the human resource personnel; and the *Transform Strategy*, led by the leaders and members of entrepreneurial teams.

SKILLS AND TACTICS

To implement the three strategies, the groups responsible must develop specific types of skills: *executive, leader, team member*, and *individual learner* (applicable to all employees).

Once these skills have been mastered, they are applied to tactics designed to implement the strategies and accelerate learning.

Vision: To sustain competitive advantage through faster learning

Strategies: To realize the FLO vision

Surge	Cultivate	Transform
Executives	Human Resource Personnel	Leaders and Members of Entrepreneurial Teams

Tactics: To implement the strategies (by using methods for accelerating learning)

Skills: To develop the abilities necessary to deliver the strategies

Technology:

To support the access to, capture of, and transfer of learning

Measurement & Reinforcement:

To measure, monitor, and support progress in implementing the strategies (by using a variety of tools)

Executive	Leader	Team Member	Individual Learner
Visioning	Facilitating group process	Applying technical competence	Questioning, listening, reflecting
Facilitating strategic dialogue	Collaborative coaching	Contributing as a team member	Reading, writing, computation
Action modeling	Managing change	Leading teams	Leveraging knowledge
Mental modeling	Strategic thinking	Running a micro-business	Learning how to learn

The FLO Model

TECHNOLOGY

Implementing the FLO Model is a complex undertaking. The organization must rely heavily on technology to support its access to, capture of, and transfer of learning. It's important to remember, though, that technology is an adjunct to faster learning, not the driving force behind it.

MEASUREMENT AND REINFORCEMENT

Implementation of the FLO Model needs to be continually monitored, measured, and reinforced. Otherwise, motivation, commitment, and improvement will not survive. A variety of tools are used to gauge and support progress in implementation.

Example: NASA

On October 4, 1957, the U.S.S.R. launched the world's first satellite into orbit. The U.S. also "went into orbit"—a virtual state of shock.

After a flurry of Congressional hearings and committee meetings, President Dwight D. Eisenhower submitted a bill recommending creation of a National Aeronautics and Space Administration.[4]

However, in May, 1961, NASA received its real spur to action. As Andrew Chaikin states in *A Man on the Moon,* "[President John F. Kennedy] stood before a joint session of Congress, and in the calmest of words...stated the unimaginable: 'I believe this nation should commit itself, before

UPI/Bettmann

President John F. Kennedy

this decade is out, to landing a man on the moon and returning him safely to the earth.'"[5]

Inspired by these words, NASA accelerated its journey toward this vision. This was an unparalleled technological challenge. But just as important was winning the competition with the Soviets in space.

And so, without realizing it (and, unfortunately, without being able to sustain it, as Chapter 8 will explain), NASA became a FLO. All the compelling internal and external forces were there:

♦ Openness to exploration (learning)

♦ An industry in which the ground rules had suddenly changed

♦ A competitive challenge—and the competition was already learning faster

♦ Stimulating leadership (providing challenge and support)

♦ A clear and compelling vision

♦ Full commitment of resources to support the vision

♦ Dedicated faster learners who were willing to put forth enormous effort and take risks to fulfill the vision

♦ A spirit of entrepreneurialism (adventure)

♦ A market (the U.S. taxpayer) that placed high value on the product and was willing to pay for it

♦ Opportunities to spin off the innovations

NASA

In the 1960s NASA met an enormous challenge: putting a man on the moon by the end of the decade.

It could be argued that NASA is not a private enterprise. NASA doesn't have to deal with the exigencies that face the corporate world. Its access to capital, for example, far exceeds that of most corporations. Moreover, the grand vision that it pursued—landing someone on the moon within a decade—could never be equaled in private enterprise.

Admittedly, the differences are significant. However, many of the dynamics that drove NASA can be, and have been, duplicated in the corporate world. The scale may be smaller, but the kind of motivation and commitment that NASA generated sprang from its need to learn faster than the competition in order to fulfill its vision. The reality that NASA faced in the 1960s is the same reality facing the corporate world today.

ACTION IDEAS

1. In your next conversation at work, share the notion that the only way to gain and sustain the competitive edge is to ensure that your organization is learning faster than the competition. Make sure that the people you're talking to understand the concept and have time to reflect on it. Then challenge them to suggest a strategic idea that would be superior to faster learning. If they can't, work with them to figure out how you might implement faster learning.

2. Ask a coworker who's involved in learning something on the job what he or she would do if only half the normal time were available to achieve that learning goal.

3. Think about something that you have to learn in the next few weeks. Plan to do it in half the time you would normally spend. After your learning, figure out how you could apply the method(s) you used to other learning goals.

4. Run the following Quick Test for a Faster Learning Organization (FLO) with one or more coworkers. The test gives you a rough idea about how your company stands as a FLO. Read the items to the respondents and ask each to rate each characteristic on a scale of 1 to 5 (1 = Low, 5 = High).

Quick Test for a Faster Learning Organization (FLO)

OUR ORGANIZATION...

❏ Assesses its strategic situation realistically

❏ Has a clear and motivating vision of itself as a FLO

❏ Responds quickly and effectively to competitive conditions

❏ Quickly converts information into valuable knowledge

❏ Has technology that's up-to-date

❏ Continually reduces cycle time

❏ Is more innovative than its competition

❏ Confidently and capably handles change

❏ Enhances its performance through both incremental improvement and breakthroughs

❏ Operates its teams as micro-businesses

❏ Outperforms its competition

INTERPRETATION SCALE

0-25: Start implementing a FLO now.

35-45: You're off and running. Work on the tactics and skills of a FLO.

45-55: Your organization is outstanding! Keep refining and fine-tuning.

Discuss the results with your coworker(s) to see what action ideas they might have to move your organization higher on the scale or to maintain an excellent status.

Summary

The only way to gain and sustain the competitive edge is to ensure that your organization is learning faster than the competition.

- ◆ All organizations learn. But the faster learning organization continues to redefine and act on its essence faster than the competition, which can't catch up.

- ◆ Employees of the FLO—executives, leaders, team members, and individual learners—develop new skills that expedite organizational learning.

- ◆ The FLO advantage derives from enhanced strategic capability, the ability to change, and improved performance.

*K*ey Idea:
A FLO is initiated by setting up a common language for communicating ideas about learning.

How Organizations Learn

Success in the marketplace today is directly proportional to the knowledge that an organization can bring to bear, how fast it can bring that knowledge to bear, and the rate at which it accumulates knowledge.

Tom Peters,
Liberation Management

2

If you want to turn your enterprise into a FLO, employees must know what organizational learning is, how it happens, what levels and types of learning occur, and what's special about FLO learning. Equipping employees with this knowledge enhances their awareness of learning and ensures that they'll be able to communicate with one another about learning.

This chapter describes the phenomenon of organizational learning, explains essential learning terminology, and differentiates the special process of faster learning from organizational learning in general.

15

Companies...are finding that the challenges of change can only be met if people are able to recapture their innate ability to learn, and keep learning on a continual basis.

To survive in the workplace—and to help ensure our company's success—we must question ourselves, gain different perspectives, and not be afraid to adopt new values and beliefs. We must reflect on our experiences. Just as when we were... children, we must always be alert to our environment and be sensitively engaged with others, so as not to miss the moments of learning.[1]

WHAT IS ORGANIZATIONAL LEARNING?

The majority of North American businesses have assumed that organizational learning is somehow related to formal schooling. But learning involves much more than studying, and organizational learning is vastly more complex than individual learning.

Most organizational learning takes place in a series of single moments that employees experience every day: contemplating activities quietly, interacting with people within or outside the organization, participating in small-group work, reading internal documents, performing tasks, watching work being done.

A simple definition of organizational learning is "figuring out what works or what works better."

A more elaborate definition is "acquiring and applying knowledge, skills, values, beliefs, and attitudes that enhance the maintenance, growth, and development of the organization."

Notice the emphasis on application of learning. Until learning is applied effectively, it isn't complete.

Let me offer a personal example. A few years ago I concluded a partnership deal with an organization in Europe—or at least I thought I had. But things started falling apart soon after I returned to North America.

I'd never met the chairman of the board of the European organization, and eventually he rejected the deal. Not until some time later did I realize that when the partnership was in jeopardy, I should have boarded the first plane to Europe to meet personally with him.

Seven years later I was involved in contract negotiations in another city. After I returned home, I found out that the agreement had collapsed. Although I initially hesitated, the next moment I called my travel agent and booked an immediate flight to my client's city.

I had to wait more than a day in a hotel room, but I insisted on seeing the client to determine what could be done to resurrect the agreement. This personal approach made a difference: The business relationship was saved.

What really happened in this sequence of events? My learning was consummated only when I booked the flight seven years after the first episode. Had I chosen not to book it, I would not have applied what I discovered seven years earlier. In effect, I would have learned nothing, even though I had acquired the knowledge during the previous incident.

It is the application of learning to the fundamental purpose of the enterprise—not the insight itself—that makes the difference.

LEVELS OF LEARNING

Another aspect of learning that's important for employees to understand is that there are five learning levels: acquisition, use, reflection, change, and flow.

1. Acquisition. The first level consists of acquiring attitudes, beliefs, values, principles, information, knowledge, and skills. A great deal of acquisition takes place before an employee is even hired.

2. Use. The second level consists of using the elements acquired. However, this use is merely activity, not actual learning, unless a feedback loop is built in so that actual performance can be compared to intended performance. For example, in the personal experience I described, I decided to change my behavior based on a desired goal (intended performance) and on feedback about how my previous behavior had prevented me from achieving a similar goal.

Work comes to depend on an ability to understand, respond to, manage, and create value from information. Thus, efficient operations in the informed workplace require a more equitable distribution of knowledge and authority. The transformation of information into wealth means that more members of the firm must be given opportunities to know more and to do more.[2]

3. Reflection. The third level requires removing yourself from the process in order to see the forest instead of the trees. Reflection is "big-picture" thinking.

Reflection is free of external action. It's marked by questioning, analyzing, and overcoming assumptions. For example, a reflective learner or group might focus on cultural issues within the organization and the effect of these issues on the way in which the business is, or should be, positioned against the competition.

Taken further, reflection might involve constructing new paradigms, which are mental models of how things work. Rethinking paradigms might mean redefining what business you are in and the way you conduct business.

4. Change. The fourth level combines thinking and action. The person or group responds to an opportunity or problem by developing a strategy, allocating resources, and taking action to ensure that the desired change results in high-impact application of learning.

5. Flow. This level is named after Mihaly Csikszentmihalyi's book entitled *Flow.* (It sounds the same as FLO, the acronym for "faster learning organization," so it's easy to remember.) In the flow level, small learnings continue to reinforce one another without conscious effort. Learning and related activity seem to coalesce in a forward-moving stream.

TYPES OF LEARNING

So far we've been talking about the learning process—the *how* of learning. Employees also need to know about learning content—the *what* to which the process is applied. As shown by the types of learning described on the next page, a great range of learning content occurs in an organization.

Any business depends on a certain minimum level of competence in task learning. Often task learning alone

> ❧ *Task Learning:* Concerns how to perform and enhance the performance of specific tasks
>
> ❧ *Systemic Learning:* Has to do with understanding the organization's basic systems and processes, how they're developed and implemented, and how they can be improved
>
> ❧ *Cultural Learning:* Centers around the values, beliefs, and attitudes that provide the foundation for working productively
>
> ❧ *Leadership Learning:* Concentrates on how to lead and manage individuals, groups, teams, and larger organizational units
>
> ❧ *Team Learning:* Has to do with how to function effectively in a team and foster its learning, growth, and maturity
>
> ❧ *Strategic Learning:* Centers around the organization's basic business strategy, how it's developed and implemented, and how it can be improved
>
> ❧ *Entrepreneurial Learning:* Concerns the basics of entrepreneurship and how to run teams as micro-businesses
>
> ❧ *Reflective Learning:* Has to do with questioning and analyzing organizational assumptions, models, and paradigms
>
> ❧ *Transformational Learning:* Concentrates on how to make significant organizational change

Types of Organizational Learning

Faster learning depends on two factors: (1) how quickly individuals and groups learn and (2) how quickly that learning is transferred to other individuals and groups within the organization.

can determine competitive standing. However, if your organization and its competitors have all achieved about the same level of task learning, the other learning types become important in gaining the competitive edge.

WHAT'S DIFFERENT ABOUT FLO LEARNING?

When a FLO embarks on the challenge of reducing learning cycle time, it focuses faster than its competition on *what* content to learn and *how* to learn that content.

It may not actually think faster. But it engages in deeper, more thorough and focused thinking that leads to more effective action. Fast thinking followed by inappropriate application leads to rethinking, which slows down learning.

To practice the kind of thinking required, ask yourself the following questions the next time you want to expedite your learning process and solve a problem: (1) What is a simple way of thinking about this issue? (2) What are the essential parts of the issue? (3) What one thing could I do that would really make a difference? (4) What would be the first step to take?

Pay close attention to both the process and the results of your learning.

LEARNING THE RIGHT THINGS THE RIGHT WAY

A critical aspect of faster learning is pursuing the "right" content and methods. Employees need to ask themselves these questions: Are we focusing on the right things to learn? Are we learning the right way?

THE FAR SIDE   By GARY LARSON

"Hey! Look what Zog do!"

POTENTIAL FOR FASTER LEARNING

Four types of organizations have the greatest potential to become FLOs:

♦ *"Greenfield" organizations:* Those started from scratch, with no previous organizational culture to burden them

♦ *Organizations in fast-paced industries:* Those in industries in which learning faster is critical to survival (for example, computer hardware/software companies)

♦ *Organizations on the leading edge:* Those that take pride in their reputations for being at the forefront of their industries

♦ *Organizations in downturn:* Those that have suffered a traumatic loss of competitive advantage and have had to scramble to find new ways of doing business

Most organizations today have gone through some kind of serious soul searching about how they're doing business. And most have decided that they can no longer do business the way they did before. How seriously they take this issue will determine their potential as faster learning organizations.

When asked why their businesses must learn, managers say the issue is simple: Learn or die. They relate examples of losing business to a competitor who outlearned them.

—Calhoun W. Wick and
Lu Stanton Leon

Example: Xerox

Xerox Corporation

Paul Allaire, Xerox CEO

At one time or another, Xerox Corporation has exemplified each of the four organizational types with high potential for faster learning: It's been a greenfield organization, it's been part of a fast-paced industry, it's been on the leading edge, and it has experienced a traumatic downturn. It has learned what works, what doesn't work, and what works better.

Xerox's founder, Chester Carlson, invented a process for plain-paper copying. His breakthrough idea launched Xerox on an exciting journey of success that lasted more than ten years. During the 1970s, however, Xerox started feeling the heat of Japanese competition. Its market share started to erode.

By 1982 Xerox was a bruised and battered company. David Kearns, CEO at the time, conceded that the Japanese were "eating us for lunch."[3]

However, the corporation's benchmarking process and subsequent quality initiatives created a remarkable turnaround in Xerox's fortune. It became the first U.S. company to win back market share from the Japanese.

Today Xerox, still committed to figuring out faster what works better, is facing new challenges. Its CEO, Paul Allaire, contends, "Xerox is now in the midst of a technological transformation that is revolutionizing our business. It is changing the skills our employees need, the competitors we face—and, indeed, the very nature of the business we are in."[4]

How is the company responding to these challenges? For one thing, it has changed its structure. The company has been split into eight divisions, each accountable for a particular product group.

Allaire is zealous about breaking down the walls between research and development, marketing, and manufacturing. A recent internal document, "Xerox 2000: Putting It Together," outlines how the new Xerox will operate.

The document identifies eight core values, one of which is labeled "Organization Reflection and Learning" and is discussed in these terms: "We achieve continuous improvement through constant learning. As individuals and as groups, we gain insight by reflecting on our successes and failures. We learn from each other, our competitors, and our customers."[5]

ACTION IDEAS

1. At the first meeting of a new project team, encourage the team members to reflect on what they need to learn to accomplish their mission. Use the types of learning described in this chapter as a discussion starter. Then create a learning plan that complements the project plan. Be as specific as possible about learning content, tasks, and outcomes.

2. Meet with a group whose principal focus has been on performance. Ask the following questions and record responses on a flip chart, using a separate sheet for each question:

   ♦ What are the key things we have learned from our organization's (or work group's) past?

   ♦ What are the key things we are presently learning in our organization (or work group)?

   ♦ What key things do we need to learn in the future?

   Lead a discussion on what might be done to ensure that the necessary future learning takes place.

3. Either on your own or with another interested person, reflect on some recent learning experience. Examine the experience from the viewpoint of how you might have learned faster than you did. The following questions might help to focus your thinking:

   ♦ What was the key thing I learned?

   ♦ How clear or unclear was I about the identity of that key thing at the time? Was it obvious or continually shifting?

   ♦ What could I have done to make that key thing clearer to me sooner?

   ♦ How did I learn? What was the process I went through?

   ♦ How could I have accelerated that process? What steps could I have omitted? What one or two things could I have concentrated on (and let the others go)?

   ♦ How could I have better used the learning resources available to me (peers, associates, my boss, suppliers, customers, and so on)?

4. Think of some learning that you will need to undertake in the near future. Plan how you will accelerate that learning.

SUMMARY

If your organization chooses to focus on faster learning, it has to develop a clear and common language about learning so that the relevant principles can be applied.

♦ Employees need to know the types and levels of learning.

♦ Employees need to understand what organizational learning is ("figuring out what works or what works better") and how it occurs.

♦ Then employees can progress to the definition of "faster learning":

Faster learning is figuring out faster than the competition what works or what works better.

K*ey Idea:*
To implement a FLO, you must encourage people
to be receptive to learning, challenge them with
change, and provide stimulating leadership.

LAUNCHING THE FLO

---

*The special openness or receptivity of 21st-century thinking
results in extremely sensitive antennae; the individual is
psychically open, will use anything as a tool to better
understand problems or the world at large.*

Marsha Sinetar,
Developing a 21st-Century Mind

3

A FLO needs a sound launching in order to travel
in the stratosphere of success. This chapter describes
the three components of a sound launching: openness
to learning, the challenge of change, and stimulating
leadership.

OPENNESS TO LEARNING

Learning is seldom easy. For many, it's a deeply painful
experience, associated with early ordeals in school.
However, we're clearly moving into a work world in
which continual learning is the norm. The workplace is
starting to replace school as the primary—or at least the
lengthiest—learning experience in a person's life.

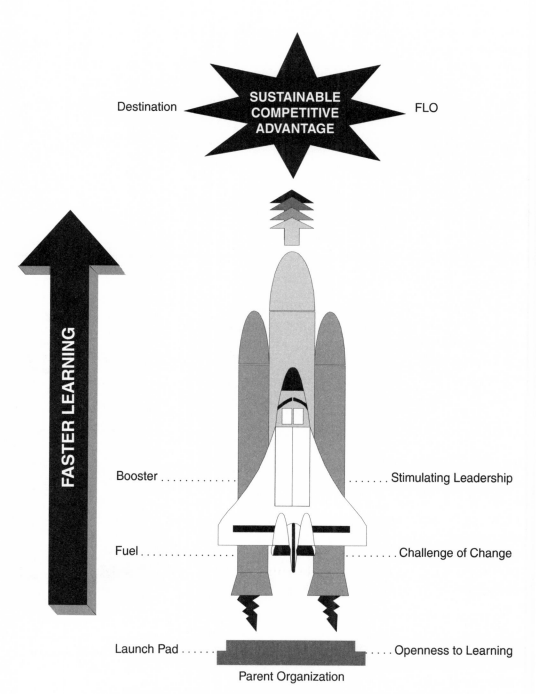

Destination — SUSTAINABLE COMPETITIVE ADVANTAGE — FLO

FASTER LEARNING

Booster . . . . Stimulating Leadership

Fuel . . . . Challenge of Change

Launch Pad . . . . Openness to Learning

Parent Organization

A Sound Launching Leaves the Competition Behind

Given this picture of the future, we need to address the pervasive phenomenon of resistance to learning. Followers are by no means the only ones who show resistance. Unfortunately, resistant leaders can damage the learning environment more than followers. Resistant leaders come in many guises:

♦ Those who refuse to support anyone's learning and focus only on today's performance

♦ Those who verbally support learning, but take no action to back up their words

♦ Those who support others' learning, but do nothing to demonstrate their own willingness to learn

A FLO demands more than willingness to learn: It demands eagerness. If leaders are not enthusiastic about learning—their own and others'—then why should anyone in the organization be?

DEVELOPING OPENNESS

Openness to learning is a product of two forces: a person's *self-image* and *the relevance of the opportunity* that the learning presents. In other words, if I'm not open to learning, my resistance means (1) I don't feel good about myself, so I don't think I can improve, and/or (2) the learning opportunity at hand doesn't seem relevant to my work, so I choose to ignore it.

Let's consider the case of a leader who's a strong supporter of learning but is faced with a subordinate who either feels unable to learn or views the learning as irrelevant. What should that leader do?

*I*f *people don't see you in the trenches alongside of them, they may not go the extra distance that success today demands.*

—Bill Walsh

THE FAR SIDE By GARY LARSON

"Mr. Osborne, may I be excused? My brain is full."

1. Share information. The leader should freely share information about what's happening in the organization. Decreasing resistance to learning is dependent on opening the company's books, explaining its vision, talking about the competitive realities it's facing and what to do in response, and discussing what each person's role will be in that unfolding scenario.

2. Offer encouragement. The learner should be encouraged to take a small first step—one that will provide immediate success and reinforce the learning. The leader might ask the learner what small act would make it easier to learn and then invite the learner to take that first step.

Enlist peers to mentor employees who need to improve. This pays off in two ways: It boosts the mentor's ego. And those who need help will value it more because it comes from someone who faces the same problems.[1]

3. Assign a reluctant learner to a team of open learners. The enthusiasm of open learners is often infectious. Team members can share their experiences and help one another to learn.

4. Exercise patience. A learner needs time to understand fully what the learning implies, to see how the learning relates to both personal and organizational needs.

> ***The leader should explain not just what needs to be learned and how, but also why that learning is important.***

There are other ways to help, too: Partner the reluctant learner with a strong one, hold small-group sessions in which each person shares learning successes, and conduct training focused on improving basic learning skills (reading, writing, and computation).

If these approaches fail, at some point a hard decision may have to be made. Some people who refuse to learn (probably no more than 5 to 20 percent of the work force) may have to be let go.

THE CHALLENGE OF CHANGE

Once people start to open up to learning, they need to be challenged in ways that are appropriate to their respective levels of confidence and competence.

Think of times when your personal learning curve soared. Very likely you were confronted with an unprecedented personal challenge. Perhaps you rose to the challenge because of a crisis or because the person challenging you was inspiring or threatening or both. In any case, you felt compelled to respond—and quickly.

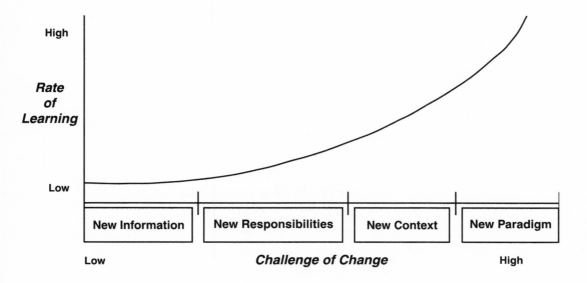

The Challenge of Change Continuum

An individual without information cannot take responsibility; an individual who is given information cannot help but take responsibility.

—Jan Carlzon

What you learned in turn required you to change, sometimes in significant ways. The experience was undoubtedly unsettling, chaotic, and stressful. Change always is. But your learning moved at a pace that amazed you, and that was exhilarating.

This dynamic is the challenge of change. The degree of challenge dictates the rate of your learning; the more challenging the change, the more your learning will accelerate. On the previous page is an illustration of the Challenge of Change Continuum. The paragraphs below explain the continuum.

A new paradigm: Merck's acquisition of Medco, a mail-order provider of drug and health benefits, completely changed the rules of the pharmaceutical game—particularly distribution. Within months, all of Merck's top competitors responded with acquisitions of their own.

1. New information. At the extreme left or "low" end of the Challenge of Change Continuum is new information. A report, an announcement of a new product, a new computer system, or a work-related discussion may constitute new information.

2. New responsibilities. The next level is new responsibilities. These might involve a promotion, an assignment to a task force or project team, expansion of your present work role, cross-training in other people's jobs, or the requirement to teach your job to someone else.

3. New context. The next higher level, new context, refers to a new situation that surrounds you at work. A new context might be a new CEO, a new change program like total quality management or reengineering, or a new set of policies and procedures. The difference between new context and the previous levels is that the new context affects everyone, not just you; it's more complex and pervasive.

4. New paradigm. At the extreme right or "high" end of the continuum, the most challenging level, is a new paradigm. What this means is that the ground rules for your business or industry have radically changed. What used to lead to success in your industry no longer works. Usually a competitor has made a bold move that the whole industry feels the need to respond to.

Learning is accelerated by moving to the right of the continuum. Meg Wheatley, consultant and author of *Leadership and the New Science,* likens moving to the right of the continuum to working at the edge of chaos.[2]

> *Great potential for significant change lies at the chaos-edge point.*

At each stage of the continuum, a different thing must be learned. With new information, it's how to do the current job better; with new responsibilities, how to do another job; with a new context, how to manage organizational change. And with a new paradigm, it's how to gain competitive advantage.

As people move to the right of the continuum, they need to master the learning from the less challenging stages. For example, if a new change program is introduced, they have to learn not only the program content, but also new information related to the program and how to perform new responsibilities arising from the program. A new paradigm involves new information, new responsibilities, and new contexts, and each of these affects the others.

STIMULATING LEADERSHIP

The best leaders for the FLO are characterized as *stimulating.* They are capable of providing not just challenge, but also support. Stimulating leaders are able to change the levels of challenge and support they provide, depending on the needs of individual employees in particular situations.

An organizational culture must be created that will sustain an environment that values various and often conflicting points of view and considers many options. The creation of this culture is the job of the leader.[3]

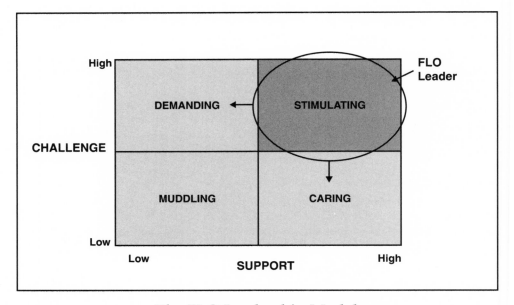

The FLO Leadership Model

Leaders who can provide challenge but not support often lack effective interpersonal skills. Their style is characterized as *demanding*. Working for them is like being on a high wire without a safety net. No one likes that kind of risk.

Leaders who can offer support but not challenge exercise a *caring* style of leadership. They don't generate an energizing learning or performance climate, and they fail to motivate employees.

And those who can provide neither challenge nor support are characterized as *muddling*. They should try to find roles that don't require leading or managing others.

CHALLENGE

Expectations help to breed results. A leader can immediately raise the level of learning and performance simply by stating high expectations of others. Of course, if those being presented with the challenge don't view the challenger as an effective leader, their response will not be as enthusiastic.

Basically, though, all of us hunger for challenge. A FLO leader must feed that hunger by presenting challenges that not only are aligned with corporate direction, but also touch people deeply.

DILBERT® by Scott Adams

SUPPORT

The FLO leader provides support so that employees can better meet the leader's challenges. This support can be manifested in several ways:

1. By providing needed assistance. For example, the leader may offer resource-based assistance, such as better equipment or extra personnel. Support also can be demonstrated by removing obstacles or establishing important connections.

2. By effectively exercising interpersonal skills. Michael Galbraith, writing about the essential skills for the facilitator of adult learning, contends that a high level of interpersonal skills is essential in developing a climate that's conducive to learning.[4] Listening, demonstrating concern, and offering any needed emotional support go a long way in helping employees to meet the challenges set for them.[5]

3. By supporting employees' decisions. Perhaps the most critical aspect of support is standing up for employees when they have made decisions—whether those decisions are good or bad. In an article entitled "Winning Trust," Perry Pascarella counsels that the

DILBERT reprinted by permission of United Feature Syndicate, Inc.

Counting on your employees to read minds...often results in disappointment and distrust. Managers feel impatient and irritated with employees who need more specific information; employees sense that they have disappointed the boss but usually have no idea what they need to do to meet expectations.... Studies show that [only] about 20% of any group of employees will be good enough at learning by observation to figure out what is expected.[7]

leader needs to stand beside an employee in the event of a mistake and share responsibility for making sure that mistake doesn't happen again.

When a mistake occurs, the leader should follow up immediately to help the employee learn from that mistake.

Together they can study the decision-making process that was used to find out why the chosen answer didn't work: What was lacking? Information? Clear objectives? The leader should focus the conversation on how to make a winning decision the next time, not on possible feelings of loss or guilt.[6]

LEADER AND LEARNER INTERACTIONS

The matrix below is useful in determining how much challenge and support to provide employees. Learners who fall in the quadrant of *low openness, low competence*

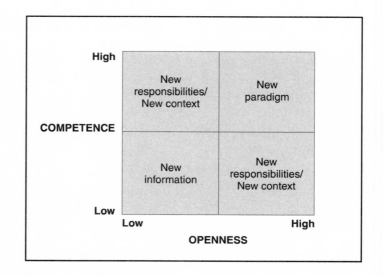

**Matrix for Determining
Degree of Challenge and Support**

can probably handle only *new information.* To challenge them with more might drive them to despair.

Most employees, however, fall in one of the next two quadrants: (1) *high competence, low openness* or (2) *low openness, high competence.* In either case they can probably be presented with learning situations that entail *new responsibilities* or a *new context.* Learners who typify the remaining quadrant, *high competence, high openness,* can take on *new paradigms,* either responding to or developing new ground rules.

Learners who are low in both competence and openness need much more support than challenge. This kind of learner probably has not only a low self-image, but also a low tolerance for significant change.

Most learners, those who are high in one dimension and low in the other, need approximately equal degrees of challenge and support. However, learners who are high in openness and competence hunger for challenge—a new paradigm that will take them to the limits of their abilities.

Example: Scott Allen, FLO Leader

In a previous position, Scott Allen was a software development manager for the Unix Storage Server at StorageTek in Colorado. StorageTek designs and manufactures information storage and retrieval products for the high-performance computer environment. Scott truly embodied the image of stimulating leadership needed in a FLO, providing both challenge and support: "We try to challenge, to push the envelope, push the capabilities of the team.... You challenge them (the team members) to meet this requirement that has not been met before." Scott and his team were never satisfied with the status quo.

Scott Allen

In terms of the support he offered, Scott saw himself as a coach—more specifically, a "mother coach." He liked the mother connotation because it offset the "mean" image that many people have of well-known sports coaches.

Scott resembled a Boy Scout or Girl Scout master leading the group on a long hike. In his group there were those racing up the trail ahead, those staying with the majority of the pack, and those straggling behind. All had to be moving forward, with the Scout master helping in appropriate ways.

Some people scorn to be taught; others are ashamed of it, as they would be of going to school when they are old; but it is never too late to learn...and...no shame to learn as long as we are ignorant, that is to say, as long as we live.

—Seneca

"What we have to do with the team sometimes," he said, "we've got to get the Windex, we've got to spray it on the windshield, and we've got to take off the mud. And we only do that by talking and seeing where we're going. Then it becomes crystal clear."

How did Scott select his team members? Chemistry first, skills second. In Scott's view, the interpersonal dimension played a greater role in team performance than the particular level or mix of technical expertise.

Two other critical components helped to drive Scott's group members as faster learners: the Mentor Program and their On-Line Project Notebooks. Each time a new person was brought in, he or she was immediately assigned a mentor for about six months and was given an On-Line Project Notebook, which outlined processes, templates, and "owners" to consult on any work issues.

What kinds of bottom-line results did Scott achieve? When I asked Scott that question, his first response was that his people had fun. But there was much more. He retained all his people for several years, and their two-year product-development cycle time was reduced to one year.

Significant process improvements also were achieved. The quality of the product improved. The test team was integrated with the development team earlier in the process. The result? A reduction in the error rate from two or three errors per 1,000 lines of code to one error per 1,000 lines of code.

And what did Scott see as the next step? How to "bottle" everything that he and his employees had learned and how to encourage faster learning in other areas of the company.

ACTION IDEAS

1. Offer your associates a story about someone who couldn't see the connection between his or her learning and future prosperity, both personal and organizational. Ask them for similar stories about employees in your own organization or in another. Then explore various ways that those failures to make connections might be overcome.

2. Ask your coworkers what gets in the way of learning in your work group. Have them identify specific personal, work-group, and organizational obstacles. Facilitate group problem solving to determine how to overcome one main obstacle from each of the obstacle types.

3. Work with some of the key leaders of your organization to develop a leadership survey concerning the elements of challenge and support. Include about five behaviors under each heading, and use a five-point scale for each behavior (for example, 0 = Never or Almost Never, 1 = Infrequently, 2 = Sometimes, 3 = Often, 4 = Always or Almost Always). Make the survey instrument available to all interested leaders in

your organization. If you have an upward feedback program (a system by which employees rate their bosses on leadership behavior), incorporate this instrument into it. The instrument also might be built into other management programs or communication programs.

4. Work with senior management to make financial and strategic information about your organization more available to employees. Then find ways to clarify and enliven that information so that it can be shared broadly and will evoke interest and support. Use that information to lead discussions on how employees could be personally affected by what the future holds.

5. Encourage your associates to develop a handbook that will orient new employees to your enterprise as a FLO and will describe how the new employee might contribute to the organization's learning.

Summary

Before entrepreneurial teams embark on the FLO journey, the following three conditions must be met:

♦ Both leaders and followers must be open to learning.

♦ Leaders must be willing to push themselves and others to "the tolerable edge of chaos" to accelerate learning.

♦ Leaders must engage in stimulating leadership, providing both challenge and support in appropriate degrees.

***K**ey Idea:*
Having three organizational units initiate the three FLO strategies not only fosters executive support, but also increases the chances for success in building and maintaining a faster learning organization.

CRAFTING THE FLO STRATEGIES

*The more the strategists reduce the time
between strategy formulation and strategy implementation,
the more current is the information they factor into their
strategies.... Because the business environment is a constant-
ly moving target, real-time strategies offer significant
advantages over outdated strategic plans.*

L.T. Perry, R.G. Stott, and W.N. Smallwood,
Real-Time Strategy

4

When strategy is designed and implemented properly, it enhances learning. Arie de Geus, formerly of the Royal Dutch/Shell Group, sees the planning of strategy as a learning exercise.[1] He reports that Shell's executives come up with scenarios that could unfold within the oil industry and then encourage their managers to design strategies that would withstand even the most unlikely and devastating changes.

Arie de Geus

Not only is Shell better equipped to handle turbulence as a result, but its managers have become sensitized to possible futures. Inevitably, imagining various scenarios and planning for them has stimulated the managers' follow-through thinking: *"If* scenario X actually unfolded, how *would* I handle it?"

The FLO is predicated on three strategies that can help any enterprise plan successfully in the same way as Shell. These three are different from other organizational strategies in several ways:

♦ They all focus on faster learning to sustain competitive advantage.

♦ They encourage organizational leaders to think strategically.

♦ They integrate faster learning into the processes of strategic design and implementation.

♦ They are led by three different parts of the organization, thereby broadening participation and increasing people's sense of ownership.

The strategies also complement—rather than interfere with—whatever organizational strategies already exist. Yet they still need to be developed as separate and distinct from what exists so that they receive the attention they deserve at the executive level.

> *Only with executive commitment*
> *can the organization concentrate*
> *its energies on sustaining competitive*
> *advantage over time.*

The three FLO strategies—Surge, Cultivate, and Transform—are illustrated on the next page. The Surge and Cultivate Strategies are explained in detail in the following paragraphs, and Chapter 5 is devoted to a description of the Transform Strategy.

THE SURGE STRATEGY

The Surge Strategy accelerates learning around a few key leverage points in order to *surge* ahead of the competition. Two crucial factors determine its success: (1) the executive group's commitment to faster learning as the primary route to improved performance and (2) a method for clearly identifying strategic leverage points and for accelerating learning around those points. High strategic leverage is what propels the organization to a sustainable competitive position.

But what if your organization is not presently in such a position? How do you get there? Here's a five-step approach:

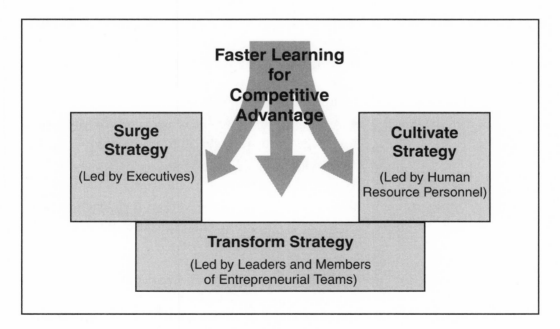

The FLO Strategies

No talent in management is worth more than the ability to master facts—not just any facts, but the ones that provide the best answers. Mastery thus involves knowing what facts you want; where to dig for them; how to dig; how to process the mined ore; and how to use the precious nuggets of information that are finally in your hand.[2]

1. Identify strategic leverage opportunities. Your organization may have a number of opportunities to gain leverage.

- ◆ A key success factor for your business or industry or a special mix of assets that the competition doesn't have[3]

- ◆ A core competence, a unique set of activities and skills in which your organization already excels[4]

- ◆ Product lines or services that your competitors haven't developed or even thought of[5]

- ◆ A particular market segment in which your organization could achieve lower cost or differentiation, or a narrow market niche that your organization could focus on[6]

- ◆ Proprietary knowledge

- ◆ An area in which your organization's key strength and its major opportunity overlap

- ◆ A development or anticipated development in the business environment that represents a unique opportunity

- ◆ A preemptive move in which your organization changes your industry's ground rules[7]

- ◆ Development of a strong strategy that anticipates a range of possible scenarios[8]

- ◆ A strategy that addresses significant values held by your organization, its customers, and its suppliers[9]

2. Select a leverage opportunity and benchmark it. Benchmarking is a measurement (and motivation) system that consists of comparing your own organization's processes and performance results against those of other organizations. A FLO adds another dimension, too: anticipating and benchmarking against future standards.

3. Develop a FLO project plan centered around the leverage opportunity. The intent of this plan is to accelerate learning about the opportunity: (1) What types of knowledge do we need to acquire? (2) How will we accelerate our learning to gain that knowledge? (3) What's an appropriate first step to start this FLO project?

4. Enlist others in strategy implementation. If a particular group has been assigned a specific task related to the FLO project, meet with the members and ask these questions: (1) If we had to complete this task in half the normal time, how would we do it? (2) What kinds of things would we have to learn before we could proceed? (3) How would we accelerate the necessary learning?

5. Monitor and measure progress on the FLO project. Once again, benchmarking is the key. As the point of the Surge Strategy is to surge ahead of the competition, you need to compare your organization's progress to the competition's progress.

THE CULTIVATE STRATEGY

A FLO requires fast learners. They are the ones who will set the pattern of beating the competition at learning.

The Cultivate Strategy falls under the purview of the human resources unit. That unit sets up a cross-functional and cross-hierarchical team, which then follows these steps to create an action plan for developing and hiring fast learners:

1. Discuss what a fast learner looks like. Team members talk about the general behavioral characteristics and skills that a fast learner in your organization should have.

2. Develop a profile of a fast learner. Team members first agree on which behaviors and skills a fast learner

Great men and women of history did not merely have superior intellectual capacities.... They had phenomenal levels of emotional commitment, motivation, attentional capacity—all of which reflected the highly integrated brain in action.[10]

Learning Levels

Flow								
Change								
Reflection								
Use								
Acquisition								

Learning Content

Matrix for Identifying Fast Learning Behaviors and Skills

should have and then use any of several methods to develop a profile of a fast learner. One method is to set up a matrix of fast learning behaviors and skills, using the two dimensions of learning *content* (knowledge) and learning *levels* (acquisition, use, reflection, change, and flow). For each cell in the matrix (see the sample above), the team members list fast learning characteristics in specific behavioral terms.

3. Rate the behaviors and skills. First the team members review the organization's vision, mission, and overall business strategy. Then they individually rate the *importance* of each behavior and skill on a five-point scale (1 = low importance; 5 = high importance) according to their

> *Measuring learning speed is as important for a company as having reliable financial data.*
>
> —Calhoun Wick and David Ulrich

importance in terms of achieving the vision, mission, and strategy. A similar procedure is then used to rate the organization's current *application* of these behaviors and skills. Again, the team members use a five-point scale (1 = low application; 5 = high application).

The facilitator or leader develops a composite rating for each behavior/skill on each dimension (importance and application).

4. Decide on a method for applying the profile. I recommend using the composite ratings attained during the previous step to construct another matrix, with the behaviors/skills assigned to the four quadrants (see the figure below).

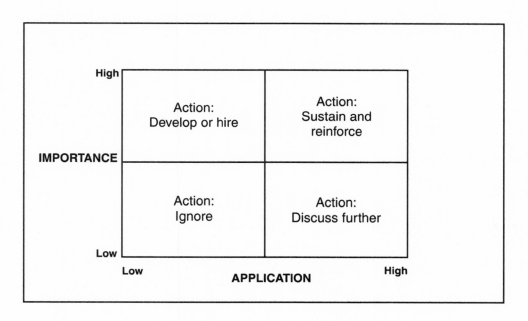

**Matrix for Determining Importance and
Application of Behaviors and Skills**

♦ *High importance, high application:* Those behaviors and skills that fall in the quadrant of high importance and high application represent fast learning characteristics that already exist in the organization and should be sustained and reinforced.

♦ *Low importance, low application:* Behaviors and skills that fall in the quadrant of low importance and low application can be ignored for the time being. However, every six months or so they should be reexamined to determine whether they have grown in importance because of changing strategic circumstances.

♦ *Low importance, high application:* The quadrant of low importance and high application houses behaviors that fast learners are giving a lot of attention to, despite the fact that these behaviors are not considered important. The team should question the reasons for this misapplication of effort.

♦ *High importance, low application:* This quadrant is the most important in terms of action to be taken. The behaviors and skills that fall within it are the ones that must be developed or hired in order to implement a FLO.

5. Design an action plan for developing and hiring people. The team establishes steps to take for developing and hiring behaviors and skills in the high importance, low application quadrant (behaviors and skills that are needed but don't currently exist).

> ***The plan should provide clear guidelines for those responsible for developing and hiring.***

6. Implement and monitor the action plan. The team should meet at least twice a year to ensure that the plan is unfolding as it should. Moreover, the entire six-step process should be repeated with each strategic-planning cycle or when a significant strategic shift is about to occur.

THE TRANSFORM STRATEGY

The third strategy of the FLO is called the Transform Strategy. Undertaken by the leaders and members of the entrepreneurial teams, it creates a dynamic for continuing growth and renewal. As the description of the teams' responsibility in transformation is a lengthy and detailed one, the entire next chapter is devoted to it.

Example: Toyota

The founder of Toyota Motor Works, Sakichi Toyoda, had a vision of an auto manufacturing company operating like a supermarket: assembling parts and producing cars just in time, thereby significantly reducing costs in order to gain significant competitive advantage.

However, it was Taiichi Ohno, a manufacturing leader in the corporation, who ultimately realized Toyota's vision. Ohno created an ideal environment for learning, one that challenged skilled workers to achieve their highest potential.

Taiichi Ohno

The Toyota production line of the 1950s and 1960s had all the characteristics of a Monty Python comedy routine. To a conventional manager, the constant atmosphere of shortages and deprivation, the attention paid to trivial matters, and the perpetual cycle of setting things up and tearing them apart and then setting them up all over again would have been madness. For Ohno, however, this was the perfect environment in which to learn.[11]

Although Toyota's strategic learning, to some degree, has now been absorbed into the fabric of North American manufacturing, Toyota has not stood still.

> Just when the rest of the world started to catch on to Toyota's lean production system, Toyota is adapting it to accommodate new workers and advanced technology.... In their never-ending efforts to do things better, Toyota executives seem almost infinitely adaptable.[12]

The Toyota production system is difficult to copy. Ohno wove technology and intellect into a seamless cultural web. But in the end, the success of the system was predicated on the faster learning environment that Ohno had cultivated:

> Ohno's sense of mission eventually pervaded all areas of Toyota. His presence lingers today, teaching, berating, peering over people's shoulders with the spirit of Toyota. People absorbed the presence of Taiichi Ohno. They began to teach themselves after the same fashion in which they had learned from their sensei. Learning and inquiry have become a way of life. Each person, to some imperfect degree, became an Ohno.[13]

ACTION IDEAS

1. Challenge your organization's senior executive group with the notion of sustaining competitive advantage by learning faster than the competition. If nobody can suggest a superior notion, then ask, "Why aren't we doing everything in our power to make this a faster learning organization?"

2. If you're a member of your organization's senior executive group, add a discussion of the Surge Strategy to the agenda of the group's next meeting. At the meeting encourage the participants to speculate on what strategic leverage point(s) can be used to accelerate learning. If there is sufficient interest, suggest that the group engage in a full strategic session focusing on the five steps in "The Surge Strategy" in this chapter.

3. Set up flip charts and felt-tipped markers in places where strategic improvising could be helpful—where quick, dramatic changes in business flow tend to originate. Gather people by the flip chart at such a critical moment, and work with them to devise a solution to the immediate crisis—a solution that aligns with the organization's strategic direction.

4. Speak to your organization's human resources unit about the need to hire and develop faster learners. Encourage the human resources people to study and reflect on the implications of the Cultivate Strategy and, in particular, on how to integrate this methodology into current practices for hiring and developing.

When an employee shows up for work, you've already purchased his or her...IQ points, or at least you have an option on them. At the end of each day, you have either exercised the option or you've let it expire. That day will never come again, and the option on that day's IQ points is gone forever.

—Karl Albrecht

5. Try out the Cultivate Strategy in one small area of your organization as a pilot project. Start by asking "What does a faster learner look like around here?" Set up appropriate measurements, pre-intervention and post-intervention, to determine the strategy's success. Make sure to document all your efforts so that interested parties can benefit from your records later.

Summary

The FLO is driven by three strategies:

♦ *The Surge Strategy,* which is led by executives, identifies and pursues key leverage points around which learning can be accelerated for the purpose of surging ahead of the competition.

♦ *The Cultivate Strategy,* which is led by the human resources unit, creates a profile of a fast learner that's used for hiring and developing people.

♦ *The Transform Strategy*, which is led by the leaders and members of the entrepreneurial teams, creates an environment that challenges and supports faster learning.

K*ey Idea:*
*The transformation of an enterprise into a
faster learning organization is a journey that
represents a new way of growing not just the
business, but also people's careers.*

TRANSFORMING THE ORGANIZATION

*Problems can become opportunities
when the right people come together.*

Robert Redford,
Harvard Business Review

5

This chapter discusses the third of the FLO strategies, the Transform Strategy. Although the other two strategies, Surge and Cultivate, promote faster learning, the Transform Strategy is what truly launches the organization on its journey toward competitive advantage. No learning curve is as steep as that of an entrepreneur. The Transform Strategy creates an accelerated learning pathway for the entrepreneurial team. It also presents the leaders and members of entrepreneurial teams with the opportunity of a lifetime: to grow their teams as microbusinesses.

In addition to describing transformation and how it benefits both the organization and employees, this chapter offers some basic but essential information about teams: how they work, how they learn, and how they can be motivated.

Team-member interdependence builds collaboration.

HOW TEAMS WORK

The essence of a team is its members' interdependence. Each team member needs the others to get the work done; a team can't succeed if even one member doesn't do his or her job.

Interdependence builds collaboration, and these two qualities lead to a high-performing team. In *The Wisdom of Teams*, Jon Katzenbach and Douglas Smith define a high-performing team in these terms:

> A small number of people with complementary skills who are equally committed to a common purpose, goals, and working approach for which they hold themselves mutually accountable.... [The team]...has members who are deeply committed to one another's growth and success.[1]

Specific leader and team-member skills have to be brought to bear on the team's work. Of course, each member also brings technical skills to the team. This unique combination of leader and member skills, technical skills, and individual personalities creates complex task and interpersonal dynamics. Managing these dynamics requires a clear team vision, boundaries, and ground rules.

HOW TEAMS LEARN

Team learning, the process that the members use to figure out what works or works better, focuses on answering four questions:

♦ Which team processes that add value for our customers need to work better?

♦ How can we make those processes work better?

♦ How can we accelerate our learning about ways to improve those processes?

♦ How can we capture our learning, document it, and transfer it to other team processes or other parts of the organization?

You might want to think of a team as having a collective brain.

THE FAR SIDE   By GARY LARSON

© 1985 FarWorks, Inc./Dist. by Universal Press Syndicate

Knowing how it could change the lives of canines everywhere, the dog scientists struggled diligently to understand the Doorknob Principle.

In this case you can view team learning as parallel processing among the members: An individual has an idea, tests it by sharing it with the other members, and receives immediate feedback from the "parallel processors." In this way the individual members stimulate one another's learning.

However, a distinction needs to be made between micro-learning and macro-learning within the team. *Micro-learning* is derived from addressing an immediate issue. No attempt is made to apply this learning to anything other than that issue.

Macro-learning, on the other hand, focuses on transferring micro-learning to other situations—parallel, similar, or even dissimilar. This more sophisticated kind of learning requires discipline, reflection, analysis, and projection.

Although employees may not label it as such, they *know* when they work for a learning organization. It provides equal doses of authority, responsibility, and respect in a work environment where people share a passion for personal and corporate improvement.[2]

How Teams Are Motivated

To encourage team members to learn together, the leader must stress that their livelihood depends on such learning. The leader also must add an air of excitement to the team's work and appeal to members in a compelling way.

What better way than to structure the team as a micro-business—delivering to its own bottom line?

Adopting a micro-business structure is a radical shift for most employees and teams. Taking full responsibility for meeting—and even exceeding—their customers' expectations and delivering a profit at the same time is a test of any entrepreneur's competence, let alone an internal team's capability.

What this reconfiguration requires is another set of skills: business skills.

> *The team needs to see its work as a whole business, with all the requisite dimensions and dynamics.*

Business skills include functional skills such as finance, marketing, accounting, and so forth, as well as strategic and systemic skills that provide the "big-picture" view.

The Transformation Journey

Many small businesses in existence today started up within parent organizations. Each of these start-ups was, for the most part, a product of serendipity. The original intent of the organization was to improve an internal service; then the service became so successful that someone saw an opportunity to offer it outside. That recognition generated the first step in spinning off the service entity as a separate business. A FLO converts this serendipitous event into a purposeful strategy: the Transform Strategy.

Most CEOs realize that to remain competitive in the global marketplace, an organization must continually improve its performance. James Brian Quinn, writing in *Intelligent Enterprise*,[3] is very clear about the implications of this corporate trend: "If one is not 'best in the world' at a critical activity, the company is sacrificing competitive advantage by performing that activity internally or with its existing technique."

Many managers subscribe to Quinn's notion and resort to outsourcing when the organization can't complete a particular activity in such a way that it's "best in the world."[4] Therefore, if a team finds itself incapable of continually improving its performance to increasingly higher standards, its jobs will become dispensable. Its work will be contracted to some outside agency that's already performing to global standards.

And, as most of us have seen in the past few years, downsizing and outsourcing put their own forms of strain on a business: productivity glitches, emotional stress, burnout, risk aversion, and erosion of team spirit.

All entrepreneurial teams in a FLO, on the other hand, follow a four-step approach to take charge of their own destiny and continually improve performance:

1. Benchmarking to industry leadership. When a team in a FLO is not meeting a world-class standard, here's what the organization does in response:

- ♦ Gives the team a reasonable but challenging deadline for attaining the standard
- ♦ Provides resources and removes obstacles so that the team can reach the standard
- ♦ Designates (or reaffirms the designation of) the team as entrepreneurial, emphasizing that it must meet financial objectives as well as the quality standard

The team's primary concern at this point is to deliver a higher-quality service to its customers, who, in most

Corning, Intel, and Saturn...guarantee that 5% of employees' work time will be devoted to ongoing training and development activities over the course of their entire work life with the company.[5]

cases, are internal. In approaching this task, the team conducts a review of its operations, focusing on improving both customer service and financial performance.

This pattern of action is followed by every entrepreneurial team in a FLO, regardless of whether the team is considered to have performance difficulties. And the organization's role remains the same, too; it commits to providing resources and removing obstacles. Continual improvement is the objective for all teams.

Consequently, every team must engage in benchmarking, which has been described as "the process of seeking out and studying the best internal and external practices that produce superior performance."[6] Benchmarking enables a team to set a specific improvement goal and to obtain information about how to do things better. In itself, benchmarking can accelerate learning.

2. Spinning off. After the team has not just reached its goal, but achieved industry leadership, it has earned the right to offer its services outside the parent organization.

The team needs to put together and present the executives with a convincing business and marketing plan—a plan to go it alone in the external marketplace. Usually a team at this stage needs help in crafting its plan. The team members can draw on the knowledge of people in finance, accounting, and marketing to construct the necessary pro formas. Developing a business plan is a powerful learning experience for the team.

An important component of the plan is a fixed timeline for achieving financial independence from the parent organization. The team members have to know that at some point the apron strings are going to be cut, and they will have to make it on their own.

If the executives approve the business plan, then a few key team members form the nucleus for the new enterprise. The rest of the team continues to provide high-quality service to internal customers.

It might be advisable for the external portion of the team to ally itself initially with an outside marketing/distributing concern. Such an alliance represents an intermediate step between depending on the parent organization and operating as an independent entity.

> *It's essential that the team members*
> *have a piece of the action—that they*
> *own part of the new business.*

The reality of being partial owners will drive the team's motivation, performance, and commitment to make the business succeed. The parent organization and the team can work together on how to structure ownership in a mutually beneficial way.

3. Reconfiguring the business. Over time, as the team tries to carve out a small, independent niche in the world marketplace, it will inevitably have to reconfigure what it is doing. The leaders, as they experience ever-changing global dynamics, will become increasingly sophisticated about emerging market needs and how to address those needs.

Going through this reconfiguration requires developing yet another set of skills: standing outside the business and looking at it realistically. This kind of detachment is challenging to people who have put their hearts and souls into an enterprise. Chapter 7 describes this set of skills, known as "strategic-thinking" skills.

4. Mentoring other entrepreneurial teams. The final step is mentoring. The leaders return to the parent organization as mentors to other aspiring entrepreneurial teams.

The mentors, who either contract for part-time, temporary assignments with the parent organization or come back permanently, share their expertise with teams in the early stages of development. This "closing of the loop" provides a rich learning experience for both the mentors and the members of the new entrepreneurial teams.

Learning During Transformation

Transformation and the Challenge of Change

Let's reconsider the Challenge of Change Continuum described in Chapter 3. We can trace a team's transformation along that continuum. Initially, the team members are challenged by *new information*; they learn team-member and leader skills. Then they move quickly into *new responsibilities* as they configure their team as a micro-business. The team's most critical new responsibility is bottom-line accountability.

Next the team benchmarks itself against the competition. Benchmarking presents a *new context* for performance improvement: external standards rather than just internal ones. The team starts comparing itself to global competitors.

Then, as the team spins off as a separate entity, it grapples with new ground rules. Competing in the global marketplace introduces a *new paradigm*, and the team's learning curve is now at its steepest ascent.

Transformation and the Levels of Learning

Now if we review the five levels of learning described in Chapter 2—acquisition, use, reflection, change, and flow—we can see how the team accelerates its learning development as a result of the transformation process. The team moves quickly through the *acquisition* and *use* levels.

However, it runs into a number of obstacles as it tries to reconfigure itself to align with the changing demands of the market. At this point the leaders engage in *reflection*, considering the core competencies of the team and its greatest market opportunities. When the team decides on a plan of action, it undergoes a *change* process, turning itself into the business it needs to be.

The leaders reach the highest learning level, *flow*, when they return to the parent organization to serve as mentors. The accelerated learning that typifies entrepreneurial teams as they complete their transformational journey keeps the organization at the forefront of its industry.

GROWING BUSINESSES AND CAREERS

BUSINESS GROWTH

There are a lot of organizations today that need healing. The transformational journey of the FLO fosters both health and growth by spinning off advanced entrepreneurial teams as micro-businesses. Here are some of the many organizational benefits of transformation:

♦ Motivating employees whose morale has been severely damaged by downsizing

♦ Increasing productivity

♦ Taking advantage of opportunities in global market niches

♦ Tapping into the organization's richest asset—its collective intelligence and know-how

♦ Creating a competitive edge

♦ Building loyalty

♦ Promoting organizational growth in a way that makes sense

CAREER GROWTH

The organizational benefits of transformation are only part of the story. When confronted with change, an

Today's entrepreneurs comprehend completely that information is the link between people and productivity. Digitized information has become the lingua franca of our time. Transmitting that precious cargo is as critical to our economy today as the galleons transporting gold were to the economy of 16th-century Spain. Says Howard Stevenson of Harvard: "Any business that can provide or take advantage of data transmission is in a very powerful competitive position."[7]

employee often wants to know "What's in it for me?" The FLO has appealing answers.

A current business trend—and one that seems likely to stick around for a long time—is the movement away from jobs and careers *within* organizations. Employees are advised to think of themselves as independent businesspeople whose primary relationships are developed within their professional fields. A particular firm represents only a temporary stay on the way to the next professional stop.

The bond of loyalty between individual employee and organization no longer exists.

> *Every employee's first loyalty now
> is to his or her own career.*

The FLO, however, turns what may seem like a bleak picture into an attractive option:

♦ New hires are told that their career paths will not be "up" the organization, but "out" the organization and into another venture.

♦ The organization bases its hiring of employees, in part, on their ability to learn faster and their eagerness to become part of an entrepreneurial team.

♦ Training and development focuses not only on technical, team-member, and leader skills, but also on business skills.

♦ Benchmarking to "best in the industry" or "best in the world" becomes a way of life for employees.

♦ Spinning off with an entrepreneurial team becomes the goal of most, if not all, employees. People can be assured that their teams will be both challenged and supported in that opportunity.

♦ When a team is spun off, the members know that each of them will hold a piece of the new entity and that they will be given a significant opportunity.

♦ As a team carves out a narrow niche for itself in the global marketplace, the leaders will have an opportunity to hone their skills further by reconfiguring the business as necessary.

♦ In the culminating act of their careers, the leaders will serve as mentors to new entrepreneurial teams in the parent organization.

Example: American Airlines and SABRE[8]

An American Airlines legend recounts the chance meeting of two Mr. Smiths on a Los Angeles-to-New York flight in 1953. One was the president of American Airlines and the other a senior sales representative for IBM. The outcome of the encounter was a data-processing system that creates complete passenger records and makes them available at any American Airlines location. Not only did SABRE (Semi-Automated Business Research Environment) enable American Airlines to link a passenger name to a specific seat sold, but it also made it possible for American to link to other airlines' passenger inventories.

SABRE was initially designed to better service internal clients, namely reservations personnel. However, as the system became more sophisticated, the idea of offering SABRE outside the airline—to travel agents—began to take shape. By 1975 American was selling SABRE to travel agencies across the U.S.—a true entrepreneurial team spin-off. From that point on, SABRE was transformed a number of times to meet the ever-changing needs of the marketplace and to expand its ability to service other markets.

What started as an internal service improvement ended up as a stand-alone business that's currently generating approximately $1.5 billion in revenue a year.

Today SABRE is the largest privately owned, real-time computer network and electronic distribution system in the world.

And, as happens in every organization, the original entrepreneurial team has developed its own culture. One of SABRE's senior managers contends, "We've gone through a total learning curve. The airline has their way of doing things. We are a totally different business."[9]

Recently American initiated another entrepreneurial team spin-off, the AMR Training & Consulting Group. American has obviously learned how to capitalize on the power of entrepreneurial teams.

ACTION IDEAS

1. Develop a list of potential or real teams. If all teams don't come to mind readily, use a current organizational chart. Rank the teams in order according to how competitive they are within your industry or globally (1 = most competitive). In other words, if any of them were spun off as separate entities, which would be most ready to compete in the global marketplace? Share and discuss your assessment with at least one other person at work. Or have the other person do his or her own ranking; then compare the two sets of results.

2. Approach senior management with your ideas on the Transform Strategy and how it might apply to your organization. Suggest initiating a pilot program. You might recommend a team to start with based on the analysis from the first action idea.

3. Talk to your training department or function about what it has to offer in business-skills training. Share your ideas about entrepreneurial teams and the need to train teams in business skills. Also, suggest that the training incorporate strategic/systemic analysis that

allows the team to do two things at the same time:

♦ Address real strategic and operational issues that the team is facing now

♦ Learn a procedure for conducting a strategic/systemic analysis so that the procedure can be applied to other business problems and opportunities

4. Speak to someone in your finance or accounting department about how to structure a financial model that could clearly demonstrate a bottom line for each team in the organization as well as each team's contribution to the organizational bottom line. Let the person know that you recognize this is not an easy task, but that this information is critical in establishing entrepreneurial teams.

SUMMARY

The Transform Strategy establishes entrepreneurial teams and sends them on a transformational journey.

♦ Entrepreneurial teams operate as micro-businesses, initially offering benchmarked, higher-quality services to internal customers, but eventually offering those services to external customers within a narrow global market niche.

♦ Spinning off entrepreneurial teams is a new way to grow businesses.

♦ Moving *out* of the organization rather than *up* represents a new career path for workers.

K*ey Idea:*
Faster learning tactics act as a bridge between strategies and skills. Use of the tactics alone can ignite sparks of learning throughout an organization.

HITTING WARP SPEED

Learning and speed feed on each other and become a development "breeder reactor." (A breeder reactor is a nuclear reactor that produces more fuel than it uses.)

Christopher Meyer,
Fast Cycle Time

6

Learning, like change, can occur in small increments or in huge leaps called breakthroughs. This chapter describes the faster learning tactics that facilitate both incremental and breakthrough learning.

EMPLOYING LEARNING TACTICS

Tactics that increase learning effectiveness and efficiency include lifting a level, eliminating "learning float," sliding a stage, going to the source, using counterpoint learning, confronting people in "work-out" meetings, and bringing opposing groups together.

1. Lift a level. Employees need to feel comfortable at each of the five learning levels. Many, however, become too comfortable at the lower levels (acquisition and use) and are reluctant to try the higher levels (reflection, change, and flow). Functioning exclusively at lower levels can be detrimental to both the employee and the organization. Consider, for example, the ramifications of never *reflecting* on how to do your job better.

Lifting to a higher-than-customary level of learning is a challenge. To meet this challenge, employees need an environment of trust in which they can fail and then try again. They need to be encouraged, to be given resources, to have obstacles removed. They need the challenge and support that are provided by stimulating leadership.

2. Eliminate "learning float." The term "learning float" means learning that's "floating out there somewhere"—not yet finished, stuck between or within levels, or shunted aside because other things got in the way.

How do you deal with this phenomenon? Suggest that each entrepreneurial team put together a learning plan based on the following questions. The team members answer these questions not only at the beginning of a project, but also at predetermined times after that, to make sure they're on the right track.

♦ What is the intended learning outcome?

♦ Who needs to do the learning?

♦ What is the learning task?

♦ How much time will be allocated for the task?

♦ What resources will be required?

♦ How could we learn what has to be learned in half the normal time?

Many people *see* opportunity...but they don't *seize* it. Seizing opportunity takes a greater step of faith. It also requires a plan because opportunity often is more illusive than the tasks you face at the moment.

You have to find a way to link the present situation with the opportunity that is before you. *You can't just sit at a desk and think positively about something and expect it to happen.*[1]

3. Slide a stage. This tactic refers to the DIFPATT Model. The illustration below explains the acronym DIFPATT. You can remember the model by thinking of the phrase "Differentiate the Pattern." The stages in the model represent different activities that require different kinds of learning: Develop, Investigate, Figure out, Plan, Apply, Test, and Transfer. In many jobs, people *apply* their knowledge or skills but don't venture into other stages.

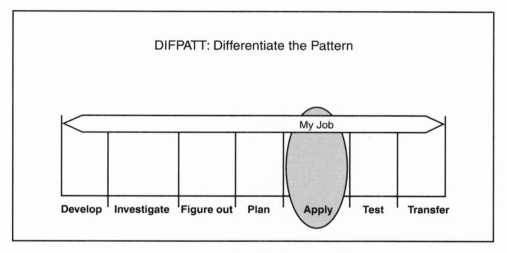

The DIFPATT Model

Participating in project teams
provides an ideal opportunity for people
to work through all stages, enhancing
their learning effectiveness.

They have to *develop* a focus for a project, *investigate* and gather information and resources, *figure out* solutions based on their investigation, create a project *plan, apply* that plan by taking action, implement a monitoring/feedback system to *test* the application of the plan, and *transfer* their learning to others outside the team.

To get people to venture beyond their normal activities, the leader can involve them in investigatory work. Generally, the information gathered is so important to the team that the investigators develop a deep sense of making a contribution, which motivates them to experiment with other stages.

4. Go to the source. Find out who's the best source of the needed data, information, knowledge, or wisdom and go directly to that individual. Even if the person is powerful, busy, distant, or difficult to approach, do it anyway.

If the source is nearby, go to that person's office. If he or she is in another facility, pick up the phone and call. (You can use e-mail if you have to describe a problem in detail, but be aware that it gives the recipient an opportunity to postpone replying.)

Keep in mind that most people don't like to turn down a request for help. In fact, many find it flattering.

> *Senior executives can promote the appropriate environment by being open and helpful themselves and by insisting that others do the same.*

Regis McKenna, high-tech marketing consultant, counsels companies not to get bogged down in extensive market research, but to make a best guess and try an initial product. Only when your customers have used a product and provided feedback on it can you figure out how to make the "right" product.

5. Use counterpoint learning. Counterpoint learning is eliciting feedback repeatedly from a knowledgeable person until you've achieved understanding. Each successive attempt brings another round of feedback that gets you closer to the mark. Counterpoint learning is similar to the slogan "Ready, fire, aim": You make quick hits around a target. An initial foray, followed by feedback, gives you a better sense of the target. The idea is to arrive at understanding more quickly.

6. Confront people in "work-out" meetings. Another useful tactic is General Electric's well-known work-out procedure. The intent is for a manager and his or her people to meet and confront one another in a constructive way. At the meeting the manager commits to taking action to make things work better.

The original work-out meetings were held over a three-day period. On the morning of the first day, the manager outlined issues that needed to be addressed. Then the staff went away for the next day and a half to wrestle with these issues and come up with suggestions. On the third day, manager and staff reconvened and the staff presented action ideas.

The manager had to respond immediately and was allowed only three types of response: "Yes," "No" (with an explanation), or "I'll have an answer to you within thirty days."

7. Bring opposing groups together. Many work groups don't see eye to eye with other groups. Sales and manufacturing, for example, seem to have an antipathy to each other.

These different perspectives are a product of the nature of the work and the types of people attracted to that work. As a result, different subcultures start to develop. Although these subcultures build internal bonds, they can obstruct cross-functional and process-focused work.

When a FLO brings naturally opposing groups together to accomplish a change initiative, their work toward a common goal creates a dynamic that I call the "accelerator effect." The facilitator acts as a catalyst, using constructive contention to generate new ideas quickly. The resulting learning can be powerful.

> **Not only can good work be done, but a whole new working relationship can be forged.**

The latest version of "work-out" is the Change Acceleration Program (CAP). It focuses on transforming the GE manager's role into that of change agent. Noel Tichy and Stratford Sherman, authors of *Control Your Destiny or Someone Else Will*, report, "The idea behind CAP is to disseminate to top management all GE's accumulated knowledge and wisdom about the change process itself: how to initiate change, how to accelerate it, and how to make it stick."[2]

MAKING THE MOST OF LEARNING

An organization makes the most of its learning by marking the miss, capturing the gain, using reverse learning, retaining the learning, and transferring the learning.

MARK THE MISS

Facts are friendly. Facts that tend to reinforce what you are doing and give you a warm glow are nice, because they help in terms of psychic reward. Facts that raise alarms are equally friendly, because they give you clues about how to respond, how to change, where to spend the resources.

—Irwin Miller

A business associate of mine once commented that he could never trust a businessperson who had *not* failed. I inferred that only someone who has experienced both success and failure can develop the judgment required to make tough business decisions. Such a person has, through a full range of experience, constructed a more accurate yardstick to use in measuring business situations.

Confronting a failure and figuring out what went wrong can be difficult within the framework of organizational politics. But it's essential to improvement.

The DIFPATT Model discussed earlier can be used to mark the miss. The team members conduct a "post-mortem" by asking themselves a series of questions:

♦ **Develop:** How did we *develop* the idea for this project? How could we have developed it better?

♦ **Investigate:** How did we do the necessary *investigation?* How could we have done it better?

♦ **Figure out:** How did we *figure out* conclusions, solutions, answers based on our investigation? How could we have done a more effective or efficient analysis?

♦ **Plan:** How did we put our *plan* together? How could we have planned better?

♦ **Apply:** How did we *apply* our plan? How was action taken? Were people clear about what had to be done? Did they know how to do it? Was action delayed? How could we have applied our plan more efficiently and effectively?

♦ **Test:** What kind of monitoring/feedback system did we put in place to *test* our plan and its application? Did it work? What might have worked better?

♦ **Transfer:** Have we *transferred* our learning from this project to other people who could benefit from it? If not, why not? If so, how did we do it? How could we do it better?

CAPTURE THE GAIN

When a learning gain has been made, the worst thing that can happen is to lose it. If initial learnings aren't solidified, employees are forced to learn them again. A FLO needs to ensure that any gain in learning is captured, analyzed, retained, and transferred.

> *Capturing requires attending to the learning while it's happening.*

Keeping a log of personal learning or team learning is good for this purpose. The log can simply be a book with blank pages, in which entries can be made at any time, or it can be a computer database. A structured log might include the date, a description of the learning, evidence of the learning, potential application, and the next step to be taken.

Use Reverse Learning

Reverse engineering consists of pulling apart a competitor's product and analyzing it to determine what it's made of, how it was made, and what its component parts probably cost. If the competitor's product is superior to one's own, the decision is made to duplicate the product—at lower cost—or to improve on it.

Reverse learning consists of analyzing a successful learning process in a similar way: How did we learn? What were the learning steps we took? What have we learned about learning? How could we learn even more effectively?

Analyzing learning "wins" reinforces the learning method used and celebrates its success.

Retain the Learning

Lessons learned reside within the collective memory, experiences, skills, knowledge, culture, structure, and systems of an organization. Organizational learning is retained by documenting that learning and retaining key learners.

Documenting Learning

Learning documentation is still rare, largely because technology is not used to best advantage. Organizations are beginning to venture into multimedia teaching/learning systems, but not many have developed computerized group memory.

If structured properly, group memory can be accessed to reveal (1) stored information, organized and sorted in any number of ways, (2) who, or what department, has the needed information, (3) timely updates to information, from creators and users, (4) lessons from similar projects conducted in the past, and (5) context: archives and stories about the company's history.

Retaining Key Learners

Another way to retain learning is to ensure that your key learners stay with the organization. One of the reasons downsizing has not reaped the productivity dividends hoped for is that the best learners, who have anticipated the bloodshed, have been the first to leave.

> *The best learners are kept by continually reconfiguring the organization to prepare it for its future, not by radically down-sizing and inadvertently throwing out the organization's greatest asset.*

TRANSFER THE LEARNING

In most organizations, transfer of learning is accidental. Few formal or even informal systems are employed to move learning from one individual or one part of the organization to another.

Here again, technology can play an important role. One type of software that can enhance transfer of learn-ing is *Lotus Notes,* a program that "takes the processors and electrical connections of a computer network and makes them work like synapses in a vast collective brain."[3]

However, technology alone is never the complete answer to anything as complex as learning transfer. Tom Peters, in *Liberation Management,*[4] cites an intriguing human system for transferring learning: A British infor-mation-systems house uses a "flying squad" of twelve people. Each person is used to "move from project to project in an ongoing quest for useful knowledge that can be turned into products with widespread utility." The squad's main task is to codify ideas.

A stumbling block to transferring learning, even within the same company, is the "not-invented-here" syndrome. One antidote to that syndrome is encouraging employees to invent new ways of implementing an idea from another part of their own organization.

CREATING UNIQUE CIRCUMSTANCES

A FLO needs to watch for and create unique circumstances, situations, and gatherings that offer opportunities for learning. To take advantage of opportunities, your organization can cross-pollinate, work the periphery, and share the fun of learning.

CROSS-POLLINATE

Probably your organization has already recognized the value and financial payoff of cross-functional teams. If it hasn't, encourage it to. The variety within such teams not only promotes learning, but also contributes to a more holistic and systemic view of the organization.

Other kinds of gatherings, such as strategic alliances and networks, can provide valuable experiences in faster learning. The simple but elegant notion of viewing corporate boundaries as encompassing both suppliers and customers breeds fertile thinking. Some companies, notably high-tech ones, are even entering into partnership with competitors to speed their application of learning.

Faster learning organizations search for and construct unique gatherings.

You might consider rotating project-team members, continually reconfiguring teams, embracing diversity, and working the Internet.

The resulting exchange of ideas, views, and assumptions keeps employees open to learning and provides insights into whole new ways of doing things.

WORK THE PERIPHERY

Joel Barker, author of *Future Edge*,[5] has pointed out that paradigm shifters are often found on the fringes or the periphery of a discipline. The fact that they have one foot inside and one outside the periphery gives them a unique perspective.

Ray Kroc was initially on the periphery of the fast-food business. He discovered McDonald's while selling milkshake machines. At the original McDonald brothers' hamburger establishment he found customer lineups unlike any he'd seen. Moreover, the quick, efficient service mesmerized him. He simply had to speak to the brothers about what they'd accomplished.

Although Kroc had seen hundreds of restaurants and knew something about the business, he'd never run a restaurant. His peripheral perspective made him appreciate and value what others hadn't even seen: that replicating the McDonald's magic by franchising it would be an entrepreneurial coup.

McDonald's Corporation

Working the periphery— partnering, questioning, and listening at the boundaries of your field or organization—holds great promise for faster learning. Barker suggests that certain people on the periphery are particularly worth contacting and *The first of Ray Kroc's McDonald's restaurants, Des Plaines, Illinois, 1955*

cultivating: young people fresh out of training, older people shifting fields, tinkerers, and mavericks.

SHARE THE FUN OF LEARNING

Learning is not always painful. At its best, it's great fun. Having fun, especially with others, opens people to learning and creates a relaxed atmosphere in which new ideas thrive.

At National Semiconductor, teams get together to devise skits portraying their units' "best practices." The skits are presented at large rallies. Not only is the skit format an entertaining, vivid way to learn; it also cross-pollinates.

Here's an example from my experience in preparing to write this book. When I realized how much reading I had to do, I was overwhelmed. One Sunday, however, I had an idea. On Monday morning I started phoning various executives I knew around town. I told them I wanted to share an exciting proposal:

> I have to do a lot of reading in order to write my book, and I need help. What if you read one assigned book a month over the next five months and summarized your reading in three clear, substantiated points that relate to creating faster learning organizations?

The executives waited to find out what was in it for them. So I continued:

> What if ten other people do the same thing? And they fax their summaries to you at the end of the month. And you fax your

Calvin and Hobbes   by Bill Watterson

summaries to them. So for every book you read and summarize, you get ten other summaries. Is that worthwhile?

Moreover, what if those who are willing and able got together once a month to share findings? Wouldn't that be fun?

And what if I arranged for all of us to share our ideas about how to create faster learning organizations using an electronic bulletin board? Wouldn't that be even more fun?

Twenty-four hours later, the FLO Reading Network had been created. I got the help I needed, and the networkers learned and enjoyed the experience. Faster learning is facilitated by an exciting, joyful environment. Faster learners continually look for opportunities to have fun in learning and to share that fun.

Example: A Forest-Products Firm

A large pulp-and-paper mill had gone through a downsizing that left a lot of scars. Now the mill was about to embark on another downsizing. This time everyone wanted to see the process handled in a more humane way. However, union and management, traditional adversaries, could not agree on how to make this happen. Finally, someone suggested forming a union-management committee and using a facilitator.

First the committee viewed Joel Barker's video *Discovering the Future: The Business of Paradigms.* Afterward the facilitator asked the committee members to substitute "game" for "paradigm." Then they were asked to describe the change game that they (union and management) had been playing for the last forty years. The committee members named that game "The Battleground."

After discussing how business conditions had changed, the committee members realized that the old game didn't work anymore. What, then, would be the guidelines for playing the new change game? Their responses included cooperation, corporate values such as recognizing the dignity and worth of employees, job satisfaction, sensitivity to the work environment, common goals and ways of reaching them, and establishing principles instead of rules. What would the new change game be called? The "People Game."

Finally, the committee had to tackle the issue of a common vision: What will an ideal paper mill look like in the year 2000? Each member developed a personal vision of the mill and posted it on the wall. Then the group was asked to identify any common patterns in the visions. Sure enough, five different elements of a common vision emerged.

Although the problem-solving and action-planning sessions that followed frequently broke down, the facilitator was always able to bring the committee members back to the common vision and the new change game they wanted to play, the "People Game."

The facilitator had acted as catalyst to the development of a new relationship between two naturally opposing groups. Union and management were now able to figure out more quickly—together—how to do things better.

ACTION IDEAS

1. Use the DIFPATT Model at the first meeting of a project team to set up the team's learning. Have the team develop a learning plan that carries through each stage of the model. At the end of the session, ask the project team, "How would we have to change this plan if we had only half the time available for our learning?" Brainstorm and prioritize the suggestions. Use the most highly ranked suggestion(s) to change the plan so that "learning float" doesn't occur.

2. Hold a mark-the-miss meeting with a group that recently experienced a failure or shortfall but has not debriefed what went wrong. Start the meeting by setting a learning context for it. State that such meetings produce significant learnings and generate ideas for improvement that will lead to future success. Make it clear that there's no intention to place blame. A framework for proceeding might look something like this:

   ♦ What was intended

   ♦ What assumptions were made

   ♦ What was achieved

   ♦ What the gap was (between intentions and achievements)

   ♦ What accounts for the gap

   ♦ What lessons can be carried forward

   ♦ How those lessons could be applied

3. Temporarily assign one person to transfer learning from one significant project, task force, or change initiative to other organizational units or areas. The guiding question for the assignment is "What

was learned from this initiative that could be profitably used by other areas of the company?" After completion of the transfer, assess its success. If it was successful, appoint one person permanently to the responsibility of transferring learning.

4. Conduct an internal learning-exchange activity: Have your team determine what recent learning it would like to share with another team. Then locate an organizational team that would like to hear about the first team's learning as well as share a recent learning of its own. Devise a sharing format and agenda; then convene the meeting.

5. Talk with people in your information-systems department about creating a group memory accessible by personal computer. Plan how people might be trained to use it. Engage the services of a systems consultant if necessary.

6. Locate a person on the periphery of your organization or industry—someone who is familiar with your business, but not part of it. Ask that person, "If you were the CEO of this organization, what would you do to accelerate learning?"

SUMMARY

Faster learning organization tactics should be spread far and wide, like seeds in a field. Then they should be nourished properly with stimulating leadership.

- ◆ Move learning to new levels by making the process simpler, clearer, more efficient, more effective.

- ◆ Challenge assumptions by asking a difficult or surprising question.

- ◆ Ensure that learning gains are captured, retained, and transferred.

- ◆ Cultivate unique circumstances that represent learning opportunities.

Key Idea:
The skills of a faster learning organization, as practiced by executives, leaders, team members, and individual learners, make the FLO strategies and tactics come alive.

Honing FLO Skills

Knowledge is the theoretical paradigm, the what to do and the why. Skill is the how to do. And desire is the motivation, the want to do. In order to make something a habit in our lives, we have to have all three.

Stephen R. Covey,
The Seven Habits of Highly Effective People

7

To reach *flow*, the highest learning level, an organization must have strong skills. Skill development is cumulative: One person's new skills rub off on another, and another, and so on. At the stage of critical mass, skills truly take hold and impact the enterprise as a whole.

This chapter discusses FLO skills according to the group or person who needs them: executive, leader, team member, and individual learner. Some categories overlap. For example, individual-learner skills overlap with all others. Also, as self-directed teams and shared leadership become more prevalent, leader skills are beginning to overlap with member skills.

Executive	Leader	Team Member	Individual Learner
Visioning	Facilitating group process	Applying technical competence	Questioning, listening, reflecting
Facilitating strategic dialogue	Collaborative coaching	Contributing as a team member	Reading, writing, computation
Action modeling	Managing change	Leading teams	Leveraging knowledge
Mental modeling	Strategic thinking	Running a micro-business	Learning how to learn

FLO Skills

EXECUTIVE SKILLS

By the time senior managers reach the executive level, you might assume that they possess all the skills necessary to be effective. In a more static world, that might have been true. In our paradigm-breaking world, executive skills must be continually reexamined and updated.

A FLO requires an executive to possess the skills of visioning, facilitating strategic dialogue, action modeling, and mental modeling.

The toughest thing about success is that you've got to keep on being a success.

—Irving Berlin

VISIONING

Visioning is a continual process of creating a view of the future and testing the present against it. The executive group must set the stage for visioning, because the FLO vision must be aligned first with the organizational vision and then with work-group visions and personal visions.

Of course, these elements can't be in complete alignment all the time. Every organization has inconsistencies. The difference between effective and ineffective organizations is that the effective ones continually address those inconsistencies.

FACILITATING STRATEGIC DIALOGUE

Executives aren't the only ones who should be involved in crafting strategy.

> *A range of interested stakeholders—*
> *from cross-functional groups to*
> *customers and suppliers—should be*
> *included in strategic discussions.*

Leading these discussions requires skill in facilitating *strategic dialogue,* an exploration of the company's strategic map or territory. The executive who facilitates this exploration works with the group in a highly interactive way: question, reflection, response, question, and so on. The discussion is highly focused and characterized by openness.

Here are some questions to get a dialogue moving:

♦ What are your ideas on this strategic issue?

♦ How do these ideas relate to achieving our vision or mission?

Business experts of various stripes reiterate: Learn how to continually "reinvent" and "recreate" yourself for success in the 21st century. Exhausting, even as an idea, looked at from the old assembly line thinking. Yet easily in the natural order of things if you commit to the new human state of the art: being a super learner.[1]

A tip for the executive: When you're explaining abstract concepts or processes that can't be observed, use metaphors, visual images, and tangible examples.[2]

♦ What's the competition doing in this area?

♦ What seems impossible to do on this issue, but if we could do it, would allow us to surge ahead of the competition?

♦ How does our position on this issue allow us to further develop or exploit strategic advantage?

The executive encourages both divergent and convergent thinking. Divergent thinking is stimulated by asking "What if?" questions. Convergent thinking is stimulated by asking "What are the common patterns or threads that have been identified so far?"

ACTION MODELING

If any executive skill is sadly lacking, it's action modeling or "walking the talk." Nothing is more demotivating to employees than to hear an executive say one thing and do another.

Many executives aren't even aware that their actions contradict their words. They can develop awareness by making a commitment with their direct reports (1) to do what they say they're going to do and (2) to do what they're asking others to do.

Members of the executive group should construct concrete examples of what action modeling would look like in practice and then meet regularly to provide one another with feedback.

Executives may need to be trained in how to give and receive feedback, a key communication skill that relates to most others described in this chapter. The principles of feedback are listed on the next page.

How to Give Feedback

1. Be helpful, not punitive.
2. See whether the person is open to feedback.
3. Deal only with behavior that can be changed.
4. Deal with specific behavior, not generalities.
5. Describe the behavior; don't evaluate it.
6. Explain the impact the behavior has on you.
7. Use "I" to accept responsibility for what you're saying.
8. Make sure what the person heard was what you intended.
9. Encourage the person to check the feedback with others.

How to Receive Feedback

1. When you ask for feedback, describe the behavior at issue.
2. Don't act defensively or rationalize.
3. Summarize your understanding of the feedback.
4. Share your thoughts and feelings about the feedback.

Feedback Principles[4]

MENTAL MODELING

A mental model, a kind of paradigm, is the product of your learning to date on any given topic or issue. It is your explanation of how things work or could work. In many cases, you may never have clearly articulated your mental models even to yourself, let alone others.

Arie de Geus coined the term "mental modeling" to describe an essential phase of planning at Royal Dutch/Shell.[3] In any organization, it is the executives' mental models that define the organizational microcosm. The real purpose of effective planning is not to make plans but to change the microcosm to meet changes in the environment, in customer needs, and so on. Executives must surface their mental models, individually and collectively, so that those models can be discussed and tested for validity in light of changing circumstances.

If your executive group is addressing a strategic issue, the following question will reveal the prevailing mental model: "How is our organization likely to address and resolve this issue?" Responses paint a picture of how things get done in the organization. The next question can lead to significant breakthrough thinking: "How could we resolve this issue in half the normal time?"

From that point on, various faster learning models, tactics, and skills can be brought to bear to accelerate learning connected with the issue.

**DILBERT ®
by Scott Adams**

DILBERT reprinted by permission of United Feature Syndicate, Inc.

LEADER SKILLS

As discussed before, FLO leadership is characterized by the ability to provide challenge and support in order to create a stimulating climate for faster learning. This leadership style requires the skills of facilitating group process, collaborative coaching, managing change, and strategic thinking.

FACILITATING GROUP PROCESS

Leadership in a FLO is facilitative. The leader helps a team make decisions by consensus, meaning that every team member has to "buy in" to a decision or it can't go forward.

Not all decisions should be made by consensus. But those that are critical to the well-being of the team should, whenever possible. People are more committed to a decision when they have participated in making it.

A consensus decision takes
longer than a leader-made decision,
but its effects last longer.

In facilitating consensus, the leader encourages everyone to contribute and question. The resulting environment of trust promotes openness, risk taking, and challenge. The team should know that both the decision and the discussion preceding it are viewed as its responsibilities.

The FLO leader never leaves a team situation without teaching the team something. After helping the team solve a problem, for example, the leader can leave behind a problem-solving model that the team or its members can use on their own.

Every team meeting is ended with two questions posed by the leader: (1) What have we learned? (2) How can we apply what we've learned?

COLLABORATIVE COACHING

To work with an individual, the FLO leader uses coaching skills. The coaching approach is collaborative: How can we two work together more effectively to produce better results?

A 1994 **University of Missouri study of 81 sales reps working for 13 sales managers showed that, of eight coaching skills, the reps scored their managers lowest on feedback, with an average score of just 6.39 out of a possible 10.**[5]

Coaching can be focused on either improvement or development. Like a facilitated meeting, a coaching session requires openness and trust. The key is the mutual acceptance of responsibility for results. If either coaching partner starts to avoid responsibility or accountability, the other must gently but firmly call him or her to task.

To accelerate the individual's learning, the FLO leader asks the same two questions as when facilitating: (1) What have we learned from this situation? (2) How can we apply our learning?

The job of team leader is an unscientific blend of instinct, on-the-job learning, and patience.

—Susan Caminiti

MANAGING CHANGE

Change begets more change. Leaders no longer have the luxury of managing change in series. Instead, they have to deal with simultaneous changes.

These are some change-management skills that the FLO leader needs to develop:

♦ Ability to link change management to strategy and systems

♦ Ability to differentiate between change as an event and transition as a process

♦ Sensitivity to the emotions evoked by change (fear of loss, for example) and consequent resistance to change

♦ Ability to apply various change-management models and diagnostic tools

♦ Ability to develop transition plans

♦ Ability to follow up and reinforce change efforts

♦ Ability to change oneself and act as a model

STRATEGIC THINKING

Strategic thinking means challenging assumptions and questioning. It means aligning routine decisions with the organizational vision, mission, values, strategy, and competencies. The FLO leader needs to focus on critical issues, high-leverage opportunities, and the long-term implications of everyday business activities.

Asking the right questions is the key to strategic thinking. The leader can use questions like these to stimulate the team's strategic thinking:

◆ What is the decision to be made?

◆ If we go strictly with intuition, what should our decision be?

◆ How does that decision fit with our overall strategic direction? How would it affect other parts of our organization and the marketplace?

◆ Does the decision still feel right?

◆ If not, what's the next best decision?

TEAM-MEMBER SKILLS

Developing team-member skills is critical to any team's success. And, as explained previously, the whole notion of organizational learning is centered around team efforts.

> *The richness, depth, and breadth*
> *of learning that come from team*
> *efforts are difficult to duplicate*
> *on an individual level.*

Team-member skills, introduced briefly in Chapter 5, need to be explored in depth. These skills are applying technical competence, contributing as a team member, leading, and running a micro-business.

North American culture reveres individualism, so learning team skills in this culture is tough. The idea of succeeding or failing as a group is a scary one.

In cultures that revere collectivism, learning team skills is much less difficult and, in fact, probably starts early in life.

APPLYING TECHNICAL COMPETENCE

Each team member brings to the team, whether it be a functional or a cross-functional team, certain technical skills (like engineering skills, for example). These are as important as any other team-member skills, and they need to be honed continually.

The organization that employs cross-functional teams exclusively may find that its people have difficulty keeping their technical skills up-to-date. Employees need to spend time with others who share their technical expertise; the resulting networking enhances their learning. One way of maintaining and developing technical skills is for each person to be a member of two teams: (1) a technical one, which is the primary, every-day work team, and (2) a cross-functional one, which is a secondary team that meets regularly but less often. Depending on what the organization requires at different times, the primary-secondary order can shift.

CONTRIBUTING AS A TEAM MEMBER

Every team must have a range of team-member skills and must use those skills for the team's benefit. Not every member needs to possess all the skills, but every skill must be resident on the team.

One skill that every member must possess, however, is collaboration, which consists of consensus decision making, conflict resolution, and communication.

The other skills might be more appropriately described as roles that can be developed in the team setting, shared, and even exchanged among members. These roles are listed and described on the next page. Team learning accelerates in direct proportion to the use of these roles and collaboration.

> 🕰 *Customer Advocate:* Keeps up with customer needs and makes sure the team attends to them
>
> 🕰 *Networker:* Knows whom to contact to get things done
>
> 🕰 *Recorder:* Keeps track of team issues and decisions
>
> 🕰 *Entrepreneur:* Comes up with new ideas and approaches
>
> 🕰 *Completer:* Attends to implementation details
>
> 🕰 *Resource:* Has information or knows where to find it
>
> 🕰 *Process Monitor:* Observes and comments on interpersonal dynamics (the "how" of teamwork)
>
> 🕰 *Focuser:* Keeps the group focused on its purpose (the "what" of teamwork)
>
> 🕰 *Fixer:* Removes obstacles and solves problems
>
> 🕰 *Trainer:* Trains other members
>
> 🕰 *Gadfly:* Keeps the team questioning assumptions

Team Roles

LEADING TEAMS

If a team has a formal leader, that leader has an awkward role: acting as a leader and a member at the same time. Some teams, however, have no formal leaders.

Instead, leader skills are exercised by different members at different times. Nevertheless, these skills are distinct from team-member skills.

> *Leader skills that accelerate learning are those that open the team to new information, knowledge, and experiences.*

For example, one leader skill involves helping the team to learn about itself—how it functions, how it creates, how it makes decisions, how it plans and acts, and how it communicates.

To exercise this skill, the team members (or the formally designated leader) may use team-survey[6] feedback and dialogue. Survey feedback is an especially useful tool. The members, in effect, tell themselves how they're doing as a team.

Dialogue is a special kind of team discourse that encourages members to speak from the heart as well as the mind. The issue that's to be the topic of conversation is presented as a short phrase—not as a question to be answered, a problem to be solved, a decision to be made, or an action plan to be developed. The intent is to explore the complexities and subtleties of the issue for the purpose of building understanding.

> *As a result of the dialogue process, members develop appreciation of the dimensions of the issue, start to sense common themes and values, or experience a deeper bonding.*

Dialogue can be used in many situations: when the team is stuck on an issue, when the members are engaged in team building, or when the organization or team is changing to a new paradigm.

RUNNING A MICRO-BUSINESS

For a team to operate as a micro-business, it needs to develop a total-business viewpoint. Five kinds of skills are involved:

- *Strategic-change skills:* Visioning, setting basic strategy, strategic thinking, strategic improvising
- *Systemic skills:* Approaching issues with a view of the team as a micro-system, interrelated with other systems inside and outside the parent organization; understanding basic business processes, such as order processing, and how they can be made more efficient and effective
- *Financial skills:* Learning how the team as a micro-business delivers to a real bottom line and how the team can leverage certain financial variables
- *Marketing skills:* Clarifying who the team's customer is and how to better meet the needs of that customer
- *Benchmarking skills:* Gathering and analyzing information from other teams or businesses in order to improve the team's performance

These business skills are best learned on the job. They can be introduced as the team works on its own business problems. As the team members come close to spinning off from the parent company, their learning will accelerate through the sheer excitement associated with running their own business.

Some countries subscribe to the importance of on-the-job training more than others. The Japanese, for example, believe that to learn new skills, learners have to work alongside more experienced employees. Guidance is provided by supervisors, but learning self-direction is emphasized. The expectation is that learners will ask for help when they need it.[7]

Individual-Learner Skills

Individual FLO learners must know that their organization expects them to take responsibility for their own continual learning. The organization can encourage learners to take responsibility in three ways:

1. Provide an appropriate learning climate. The necessary climate is developed as a result of stimulating leadership, characterized by challenge and support.

2. Recognize and reward learning. The organization's recognition and reward systems should reinforce self-learning responsibility. For example, employees can be encouraged to document their learning in individual- and team-learning logs. Although the logs are personal, they can be used as references during performance-appraisal sessions.

Also, the organization should maintain a learning profile for each employee. This document, generally kept by the employee's leader or supervisor, is filed with the employee's records. The profile should include not only formal education and training programs, but also formal and informal meetings that result in learning as well as information about desired learning.

3. Emphasize that individual-learning skills are expected of everyone. All employees, from front-line workers to the CEO, should know that the organization expects them to develop and exercise the basic learning skills discussed in this section.

Questioning, Listening, Reflecting

Learning is more a matter of formulating the right *question* than it is of formulating the right answer. If learners learn how to ask the right questions in the right circumstances, their learning will accelerate.

Although *listening* is one of the most poorly practiced skills in organizations, it's absolutely critical for faster learning. Listening requires an open, reflective mind, not a judgmental mind. It focuses on clearly understanding not just words, but the speaker's intent.

Reflection is more than a skill; it's also one of the five learning levels. Reflecting skills allow the learner to sift and sort ideas, figure things out, see the big picture, look for the high-leverage opportunity, determine what significant learning can be derived from the situation, and clarify what the next question should be.

READING, WRITING, COMPUTATION

Organizations are discovering that many employees lack basic skills in reading, writing, and computation. And, ironically, the growing cultural diversity that enriches organizations also complicates training in the basics.

Yet our expectations of employees have risen: We now want them to become knowledge workers. Without basic skills, employees can't move to higher-level skills, accelerate their learning, and meet our expectations.

Large organizations might consider offering internal training in basic skills, whereas small ones might need to work with nearby colleges that already offer such programs. In any case, there may come a time when employees need to pass tests in basic skills in order to advance in the organization or to keep their jobs. No organization can afford to keep people who refuse to learn basic skills.

One important benefit of a FLO is that its climate reinforces learning. Over time, people start taking the initiative in acquiring learning.

Literacy is being redefined for the workplace. While functional literacy relates to an individual's ability to use reading, writing, and computational skills in everyday situations, workplace literacy involves those skills and more. A workplace-literate individual is one who possesses the skills that are needed to function successfully in the increasingly sophisticated business environment. This includes such skills as decision making, critical thinking, and problem solving.[8]

LEVERAGING KNOWLEDGE

If information is the raw material of the knowledge worker, then leveraging information is a basic skill of the knowledge worker. In *Mastering the Information Age,* Michael McCarthy says, "Indeed, the challenge of the Information Age can be defined as creating knowledge out of information, getting to the essence of information, making sense of it, making it meaningful and useful...."[9] All these activities are elements of leveraging.

Leveraging information must be done within a strategic and tactical framework. One way to develop such a framework is as follows:

1. Create a personal vision. Clarify what your career path will look like.

2. Develop a personal mission. Decide the purpose you want to fulfill and the contribution you want to make.

3. Set information priorities. Determine what kinds of information will help you fulfill your vision and mission.

4. Identify information sources. Determine who and what can help you meet your information priorities.

5. Develop an information-leveraging timetable. Allocate specific times for working with various information sources.

Once you've developed a framework, you have criteria for identifying potentially valuable information. Then you need to process the information by reflecting on it, discarding parts of it, memorizing it, storing it, passing it on to others, converting it into knowledge, and taking action on it.

LEARNING HOW TO LEARN

The key to learning how to learn is to understand how you learn best—your type or style of taking in and working with information.

Learning researchers have identified different learning styles. In *Frames of Mind*, Howard Gardner contends that there is no single intelligence that guides people, but seven intelligences: linguistic, musical, logical-mathematical, spatial, bodily-kinesthetic, intrapersonal, and interpersonal.[10] Each person tends to use particular intelligences (or, for our purposes, learning styles) rather than others.

Here's an example of one of the seven. At a school Christmas concert I attended, one small boy of about six couldn't stand still while his class sang carols. He continually twisted and wriggled and didn't even bother mouthing the words of any of the songs—until the final carol. This carol involved memorized hand motions that accompanied the words. The little boy knew and imitated every one of them. Moreover, he sang along with the hand motions. He was a true bodily-kinesthetic learner.

There are also different thinking styles. Anthony Gregorc, quoted in *Quantum Learning*,[11] identifies four:

♦ *Concrete sequential:* Processing information in an ordered, sequential manner; "hands-on" learning

♦ *Concrete random:* Experimenting and using intuition

♦ *Abstract random:* Organizing ideas and information through reflection; experiencing the world through feelings and emotions

♦ *Abstract sequential:* Thinking in concepts, analyzing information, identifying what's significant

Whatever your styles of learning and thinking, capitalize on their strengths and consider developing auxiliary styles. You'll then be able to increase your rate of learning.

A tip for the learner: Immediate memory is limited to about seven "chunks" of information. Most people can remember about seven numbers in a row, seven colors, seven shapes, or seven of any other items. So if you need to remember more than seven items, it's better to organize them in a smaller number of chunks.[12]

The FLO approaches skill development as a strategic activity, and so do the various groups and individuals within the organization. Determining which skills are sharpened in which order is based on where the organization, teams, and individuals are headed. Whether skill development is undertaken as an activity separate from work or integrated with the work will depend on culture (organizational and individual), direction, immediacy of needs, existing skill levels, and the particular situation.

Example: Quad/Graphics[13]

Quad/Graphics has made a name for itself as a leading-edge printing company. Its focus on purchasing or developing the newest printing technology drives its learning. Quad's motto is "To learn, to know, to improve, and to teach."

Quad has developed a culture of simultaneous learning and teaching. Each new person hired knows that the first responsibility after being trained will be to train his or her successor. George Ryan, director of training, comments, "You don't move up until you have taught somebody your job."

Quad's executive group embodies the principles of a teaching/learning organization. The CEO, Harry Quadracci, particularly lives these principles. Once, when someone who didn't know him asked him what he did at Quad, Quadracci replied, "I teach there." Each of the vice presidents also teaches part of Quad's ten-week orientation program for new people.

Technical skills are the first skills developed at Quad. Building these skills is especially difficult when the various plants are running full tilt and workers are working overtime. But once these skills are in place, Quad can turn its

Harry Quadracci

attention to collaborative work skills: communicating, resolving conflict, building bridges, solving problems, and so on.

A regular part of the curriculum is adventure training (also known as ropes training), in which groups take a number of physical risks. This kind of training has had the greatest impact on employees who have had negative childhood learning experiences. They especially need to rebuild confidence in their learning ability.

At present Quad is concentrating primarily on developing the skills of its leader/operators. These employees both lead and do. They have the toughest job in the organization. The role of the leader/operator is to instill technical skills and the Quad spirit in new employees, who differ significantly in capabilities and motivation.

The mind, once stretched by a new idea, never regains its original dimensions.
—Oliver Wendell Holmes

One story clearly illuminates Quad's commitment to fast learning. It deals with Quad's radical paradigm shift from offset printing to gravure printing. Within three years of moving into the gravure business, Quad had become one of the leading and highest-quality gravure printers.

How did Quad accomplish this paradigm shift? First the company brought in key personnel who were technically skilled and were good *teachers*. Then it chose employees who had a real ability to *learn* and sent them around the world to work with other gravure people—those who manufactured, packaged, and shipped gravure-printing equipment. Then Quad hired a technical writer who did nothing but record and document every gravure-printing operational procedure. These tactics accelerated Quad's learning how to start and grow the gravure-printing business.

Now Quad is preparing itself for an unpredictable, continually accelerating, customer-driven future by starting cross-training as soon as possible after hiring someone. Cross-training will allow Quad's people to be reconfigured quickly in response to changing customer and technical demands. In this way, Quad is creating its own future.

ACTION IDEAS

1. If you're an executive, think of a recent speech you gave to some of your people. Reread your notes. Choose one idea that you wanted your people to work on. Now think about what you've done in recent days to model what you asked them to do. Be specific. Don't let yourself off the hook. If you haven't done anything, think of something you can do right now and do it.

2. If you're a leader, think about your next team meeting. What are you planning to do to address your team's learning? At the end of the meeting, ask these two questions:

   ◆ What have we learned about the content of this meeting that we can apply to other situations or transfer to others?

   ◆ What have we learned about how we work together as a team and how we could do that better?

3. If you're a member of a team, at your next team meeting ask the members how they think the team is doing in relation to other teams in the organization or in relation to comparable teams among competitors. If the members don't have a clear idea, suggest undertaking either internal or external benchmarking. Don't

let them squirm away from this one. Offer to initiate the benchmarking yourself.

4. As a learner, regardless of your position in the organization, continually reflect on how well you are leveraging knowledge. Read through each step of the leveraging procedure described in "Leveraging Knowledge" in this chapter. Reflect on what you could do to better leverage specific knowledge that comes your way. Consider what you could do to create new knowledge that you need. Take five minutes to put together a beginning action plan for yourself.

SUMMARY

Continual development of FLO skills is mandatory. Working on these skills is a combination of refining basic skills and moving to a new set and/or level of skills at the same time.

♦ Executives need to develop the skills of visioning, action modeling, strategic dialogue, and mental modeling.

♦ Leaders have to be capable of strategic thinking, managing change, collaborative coaching, and facilitating skills.

♦ Team members need to focus on their technical, team-member, team-leader, and business skills so they can run their teams as micro-businesses.

♦ Individual learners—all employees—need to question, listen, and reflect; read, write, and compute; leverage knowledge; and find out how they learn best.

K*ey Idea:*
Maintaining a FLO is a continual challenge that requires the commitment of every employee.

MAINTAINING THE FLO

*Technological advancements, competition,
restructuring, "me-ism," and globalization point
to the need for lifelong learning.*

Stephen L. Cohen,
Training & Development

8

Let's say that your organization has successfully completed the FLO journey. It now has a strong competitive edge and is at the top of its industry. Is it secure there? Of course not. The moment you achieve top status, your competitors devote all their energies to dethroning you.

Many organizational leaders will tell you that sustaining the competitive edge is tougher than gaining it in the first place. They're right. It's a constant challenge. But the good news is that you and your employees can grow to love that challenge, because it's exciting and because it means that everyone has to keep learning and growing. There's a special sense

Learning is no longer a luxury: It is at the heart of careers and companies determined to flourish in the future.

—Calhoun W. Wick and
Lu Stanton Leon

of pride that comes from making a meaningful contribution to a company that's the best in its field.

Tips for Sustaining Success

Here are some tips on how to maintain your organization as a FLO and sustain the competitive edge:

◆ Regularly revisit the vision and strategic framework within which the organization is carrying out faster learning.

◆ Ensure that all learning targets are challenging but attainable.

◆ Present learning tasks in a way that's realistic, relevant, and motivating. Make sure employees understand how their learning contributes to the organization's success. Also link learning to something that employees consider personally important, such as promotability or employability.

◆ Celebrate learning successes, no matter how small. Reward people who succeed.

◆ If necessary, devise and implement a full-scale collaborative-coaching plan with learners who have a negative view of their learning abilities.

◆ Ask a few people to reflect seriously on what the competition is doing and is likely to do over the next few years. Have them obtain hard facts and figures. Then encourage them and others in your organization to consider how they could be personally affected by future competitor action: How would they feel about that action? What would they be prepared to do about it?

◆ Make sure FLO targets are ongoing. For each target, choose a champion, someone who will closely monitor tasks and will convene the respective group whenever necessary to ensure achieving the target. As soon as one target has been met, set another.

♦ Continue to benchmark your organization's learning against that of other organizations.

♦ Make sure the organization is using technology to its greatest advantage for creating learning, reframing the business as necessary, and providing interactive learning as well as for documenting, expanding, speeding up, transferring, and reinforcing learning.

♦ Create the organization's future by changing the ground rules for your industry. To find clues to the future, look to "the intersection of changes in technology, lifestyles, regulation, demographics, and geopolitics."[1] These intersections are where the opportunities lie.

Example: NASA Revisited

NASA, an agency that clearly demonstrated the attributes of a FLO during the 1960s, began to atrophy once Kennedy's mission of landing a man on the moon had been fulfilled.

What went wrong? According to Jim Naughton,[2] former consultant to NASA and the U.S. Air Force, NASA's initial mandate largely disappeared. NASA became dependent on year-to-year funding and related political machinations. Although the space centers were represented in both Congressional houses in Washington, DC, no one in Congress spoke for NASA headquarters. As a result, NASA lost touch with broader national priorities and focused primarily on internal rather than external issues.

In *Inside NASA*, Howard McCurdy cites a former Apollo executive's view:

It tended to look much more like a way to divide a multibillion-dollar federal multiyear budget in a way to preserve the survival of eight or so NASA centers than a logically established program to create a national space station.[3]

Wayne Chunn[4] worked for the Air Force's Space Division Headquarters out of Los Angeles, a branch of NASA. He believes the main reason NASA is no longer a FLO is that it suffers from an identity crisis.

Today people can't agree on NASA's vision or mission. To promote international goodwill and understanding? To promote scientific inquiry? To balance the budget? To survive as an agency in the eyes of Washington? Overcome by bureaucracy and politics, NASA treats projects on a case-by-case basis, with no strategic cohesiveness to its work.

Furthermore, today's NASA lacks the support of a learning infrastructure. Although it still employs plenty of talented people who have demonstrated a strong ability to learn, it is unable to take advantage of this potential.

Chunn recounts the reasons he left NASA, sometime after the Challenger disaster in 1986. To him, NASA seemed to be slipping into a "bunker mode." He felt that NASA would no longer take risks in research—the "blue-sky stuff."

It seemed as if no one at NASA would ever again allow the agency to be exposed to the kind of scrutiny it underwent after the Challenger accident. Consequently, NASA strictly aligned itself with the government bureaucracy. It was no longer a learning organization, let alone a faster learning organization.

How to revitalize NASA? The agency's leaders have to develop a well-articulated mission and build a learning infrastructure. Moreover, NASA has to recognize that its customer is the U.S. taxpayer, not the astronauts. Most of all, NASA needs to recreate itself as a FLO.

SUMMARY

So far we've discussed what you can do to sustain your organization's competitiveness through faster learning. But a FLO also needs to address a broader kind of sustainability:

♦ How do we sustain our planet? our environment? our resources?

♦ How do we sustain our ability to improve the lives of our employees? of others impacted by our organization?

All organizations are part of the same world system. Of course we want our organizations to succeed, but we also want our employees and others to benefit from organizational success. And we want to treat our environment kindly in the process.

Consequently, a FLO needs to adapt, create, and develop a range of sustainability tools to remain competitive while helping the world to sustain itself. Because we are running out of time, learning faster is an imperative.

Notes

CHAPTER 1

1. Calhoun Wick and David Ulrich, "RAPID LEARN-ING Research Project: Summary of Findings," Wick and Company, Wilmington, Delaware, 1995. Copyright 1995 © Calhoun Wick and David Ulrich. Used with permission.

2. Janet Fox, "Conquer Information Anxiety," *Amtrak Express*, March/April 1995, p. 10. Information originally from Michael J. McCarthy, *Mastering the Information Age*, Jeremy P. Tarcher, Los Angeles, California, 1991.

3. Christopher Meyer, *Fast Cycle Time*, Free Press, New York, 1993, p. 31.

4. J. Van Nimmen and L.C. Bruno, *NASA Historical Data Book*, Vol. I, NASA, Washington, DC, 1988, p. 3.

5. Andrew Chaikin, *A Man on the Moon*, Viking, New York, 1994, p. 1.

CHAPTER 2

1. Sharon Gilchrest O'Neill, *Lur'ning: 147 Inspiring Thoughts for Learning on the Job*, Ten Speed Press, Berkeley, California, 1993, p. 2.

2. Shoshana Zuboff, "The Emperor's New Work-place," *Scientific American*, September 1995, p. 204.

3. David T. Kearns and David A. Nadler, *Prophets in the Dark*, Harper Business, New York, 1992, p. xiv.

4. Robert Howard, "The CEO as Organizational Architect: An Interview with Xerox's Paul Allaire," *Harvard Business Review*, September-October, 1992, p. 108.

5. *Xerox 2000: Putting It Together*, Xerox Corporation (internal document).

CHAPTER 3

1. "Helping Entry-Level Workers," *Communication Briefings,* August 1995, p. 2.

2. Interview with Margaret (Meg) Wheatley.

3. Ron Schultz, *Unconventional Wisdom,* Harper Business, New York, 1994, p. 156.

4. Michael Galbraith, "Essential Skills for the Facilitator of Adult Learning," *Lifelong Learning,* Vol. 12, No. 6, 1989, p. 10.

5. Ibid., p. 11.

6. Perry Pascarella, "Winning Trust," *Leadership in a New Era,* John Renesch, Ed., New Leaders Press, San Francisco, California, 1994, p. 275.

7. Albert J. Bernstein and Sydney Craft Rozen, "Why Don't They Just Get It?," *Executive Female,* March/April 1995, p. 35. Information originally from Albert J. Bernstein and Sydney Craft Rozen, *Sacred Bull: The Inner Obstacles That Hold You Back at Work and How to Overcome Them,* John Wiley & Sons, New York, 1994.

CHAPTER 4

1. Arie P. de Geus, "Planning as Learning," *Harvard Business Review,* March-April, 1988, pp. 70-74.

2. Robert Heller, *The Supermanagers,* NAL-Dutton, New York, 1984.

3. Kenichi Ohmae, *The Mind of the Strategist,* McGraw-Hill, New York, 1982, pp. 38-40.

4. James B. Quinn, *Intelligent Enterprise,* Free Press, New York, 1992, p. 53.

5. Ohmae, pp. 38-40.

6. Michael Porter, *Competitive Strategy,* Free Press, New York, 1980, p. 35.

7. Ohmae, pp. 38-40.

8. Peter Schwartz, *The Art of the Long View,* Currency, New York, 1991.

9. R. Normann and R. Ramirez, "From Value Chain to Value Constellation: Designing Interactive Strategy," *Harvard Business Review,* July-August, 1993, p. 65.

10. "Jerre Levey: Human Brain Built to Be Challenged," *Brain/Mind Bulletin,* Vol. 8, No. 9, 1983.

11. P.R. Nayak and J.M. Ketteringham, *Breakthroughs!*, Pfeiffer & Company, San Diego, California, 1994, p. 214.

12. Alex Taylor III, "How Toyota Copes with Hard Times," *Fortune,* January 25, 1993, pp. 80-81.

13. Nayak and Ketteringham, p. 223.

CHAPTER 5

1. Jon R. Katzenbach and Douglas K. Smith, *The Wisdom of Teams: Creating the High-Performance Organization,* Harvard Business School Press, Boston, 1993, p. 92.

2. Calhoun W. Wick and Lu Stanton Leon, *The Learning Edge: How Smart Managers and Smart Companies Stay Ahead,* McGraw-Hill, New York, 1993, p. 19.

3. James B. Quinn, *Intelligent Enterprise,* Free Press, New York, 1992.

4. Ibid., p. 32.

5. Lynn E. Densford, "7-Point Plan for Success," *Workforce Training News,* January/February 1995, p. 17.

6. C.E. Bogan and M.M. English, *Benchmarking for Best Practices,* McGraw-Hill, New York, 1994, p. 5.

7. Andrew E. Serwer, "Paths to Wealth in the New Economy," *Fortune,* February 20, 1995, p. 60.

8. Adapted from SABRE internal documents, "SABRE History" and "SABRE: A Classic Case History." Used with permission.

9. Interview with a SABRE senior manager.

CHAPTER 6

1. Ruth Stafford Peale and Eric Fellman, "The Power of Positive Thinking 1995," *Bottom Line Personal,* Vol. 16, No. 6, March 15, 1995, p. 1.

2. Noel Tichy and Stratford Sherman, *Control Your Destiny or Someone Else Will,* Currency Doubleday, New York, 1993, p. 209.

3. David Kirkpatrick, "Why Microsoft Can't Stop Lotus Notes," *Fortune,* December 12, 1994, p. 142.

4. Tom Peters, *Liberation Management,* Alfred A. Knopf, New York, 1992, pp. 397-399.

5. Joel A. Barker, *Future Edge: Discovering the New Paradigms of Success,* William Morrow, New York, 1992, pp. 55-70.

CHAPTER 7

1. Sheila Ostrander and Lynn Schroeder with Nancy Ostrander, *Superlearning 2000,* Delacorte, New York, 1994, p. 253.

2. Adapted from Laurie Field, *Skills Training for Tomorrow's Work Force,* San Diego, California: Pfeiffer & Company, p. 154.

3. Arie P. de Geus, "Planning as Learning," *Harvard Business Review,* March-April 1988, p. 71.

4. Stephen C. Bushardt and Aubrey R. Fowler, Jr., "The Art of Feedback," *The 1989 Annual: Developing Human Resources,* Pfeiffer & Company, San Diego, California, 1989, p. 13.

5. Marc Hequet, "Giving Good Feedback," *Training,* September 1994, p. 72.

6. See, for example, Dave Francis and Don Young, *The Team-Review Survey,* Pfeiffer & Company, San Diego, California, 1992.

7. Adapted from Laurie Field, *Skills Training for Tomorrow's Work Force,* San Diego, California: Pfeiffer & Company, p. 147.

8. Miriam Shubin, "Literacy Is Redefined for the Workplace," *Personnel Journal,* November 1993, p. 36.

9. Michael McCarthy, *Mastering the Information Age,* Jeremy P. Tarcher, Los Angeles, 1991, p. 19.

10. Howard Gardner, *Frames of Mind: The Theory of Multiple Intelligences,* Basic Books, New York, 1983, pp. 3-11.

11. Bobbi DePorter with Mike Hernacki, *Quantum Learning,* Dell, New York, 1992, pp. 122-138.

12. Peter Russell, *The Brain Book,* NAL-Dutton, New York, 1984.

13. Interview with George Young, manager of education, Quad/Graphics.

CHAPTER 8

1. Gary Hamel and C.K. Prahalad, *Competing for the Future,* Harvard Business School Press, Boston, Massachusetts, 1994, p. 44.

2. Interview with Jim Naughton, former consultant to the U.S. Air Force and NASA.

3. Howard E. McCurdy, *Inside NASA: High Technology and Organizational Change in the U.S. Space Program,* The Johns Hopkins University Press, Baltimore, Maryland, 1993, p. 131.

4. Interview with Wayne Chunn, formerly with the U.S. Air Force Division Headquarters, Los Angeles, California.

Index

About the Author

In one way or another, Bob Guns, Ph.D., has been playing the learning game all of his life—as a child, student, teacher, parent, education administrator, trainer, consultant, and author. In fact, now he's at the steepest learning curve of his life and is "holding onto his hat." He and Veronica, his wife and business partner, are living faster learning.

Once in a while, though, Bob does hang up his hat, at Probe Consulting in Summit, New Jersey. Bob is the first to admit that although faster learning has been his focus for some time now, he is only beginning to learn about it. He intends to spend the rest of his career exploring the rich and multifaceted dimensions of this exciting field. Moreover, he wants to engage with others in that exploration.

In his consulting and training with a wide variety of industries and organizations, Bob relishes addressing the challenges that different strategic and organizational issues present. Thinking clearly and acting decisively while having fun—characteristics of faster learning—make his work all the more satisfying.

Bob and Veronica plan to continue pursuing new ways to gain and sustain the competitive edge through faster learning. Bob is convinced that the future of our organizations will be based not only on how to learn faster than the competition, but also on how to develop tools for sustainability in the 21st Century.

If you want to share learning stories with Bob and Veronica or find out more about faster learning, contact them at: Probe Consulting Inc.
24 Beechwood Road
Summit, NJ 07901
Phone: 908-522-9202
Fax: 908-522-9208
INET: b.guns@genie.geis.com

THE WARREN BENNIS EXECUTIVE BRIEFING SERIES

*"To survive in the 21st century, we're going to need
a new generation of leaders, not managers.
This series is an exciting collection of business books
written to help your leaders meet the challenges of the new millennium."*

Dr. Warren Bennis
USC Professor and Founding Chairman, The Leadership Institute
Author, *On Becoming a Leader* and *An Invented Life*

Tailored to the needs of busy professionals and authored by subject matter experts, the *Warren Bennis Executive Briefing Series* helps leaders acquire significant knowledge in the face of information overload. All *Series* titles utilize the SuperReading comprehension/retention editing and design techniques made famous by Howard Berg, *The Guinness Book of World Records'* "World's Fastest Reader." Read these books in just two hours!

TITLES INCLUDE:

Fabled Service: Ordinary Acts, Extraordinary Outcomes	Betsy Sanders
The 21st Century Organization: Reinventing Through Reengineering	Warren Bennis/ Michael Mische
Managing Globalization in the Age of Interdependence	George Lodge
Coach to Coach: Business Lessons from the Locker Room	John Robinson
The Faster Learning Organization: Gain and Sustain the Competitive Edge	Bob Guns
The Absolutes of Leadership	Philip Crosby
Customer Inspired Quality: Looking Backward Through the Telescope	James Shaw
INFORelief: Stay Afloat in the InfoFlood	Maureen Malanchuk

Contact your local bookstore for all *Warren Bennis Executive Briefing Series* titles, or order directly from Jossey-Bass Publishers, Customer Service Department, 1-800-956-7739, 350 Sansome Street, San Francisco, CA 94104. For special sales or bulk purchases, call Bernadette Walter at 415-782-3122.